GIEN KARSSEN

GETTING THE MOST OUT OF BEING SINGLE

THE GIFT OF SINGLE WOMANHOOD

D0723397

NAVPRESS ◓

A MINISTRY OF THE NAVIGATORS

P.O. Box 6000, Colorado Springs, CO 80934

The Navigators is an international, evangelical Christian organization. Jesus Christ gave His followers the Great Commission to go and make disciples (Matthew 28:19). The aim of The Navigators is to help fulfill that commission by multiplying laborers for Christ in every nation.

NavPress is the publishing ministry of The Navigators. NavPress publications are tools to help Christians grow. Although publications alone cannot make disciples or change lives, they can help believers learn biblical discipleship, and apply what they learn to their lives and ministries.

© 1982, 1983 by Gien Karssen
All rights reserved
Library of Congress Catalog Card Number:
    82-062240
ISBN: 0-89109-505-5
15057

BV 4596 . S5 K3713

Third printing, 1985

(Originally published in the Netherlands as *Een Vrouw Zegt Ja*, © 1980 Buijten & Schipperheijn, Amsterdam. ISBN: 90-6064-369-0)

Unless otherwise identified, all Scripture quotations are from the *Holy Bible: New International Version* (NIV). © Copyright 1973, 1978, 1984 International Bible Society. Used by permission of Zondervan Bible Publishers. Other versions quoted are *The Amplified New Testament* (AMP), © by The Lockman Foundation 1954, 1958; the *Good News Bible* (GNB), © by the American Bible Society; the *King James Version* (KJV); and the *Revised Standard Version* of the Bible (RSV), copyrighted 1946, 1952, © 1971, 1973.

Printed in the United States of America

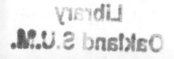

to

Margriet and Marijke
Josina and Robina
Margrieth Christine

I will open my mouth. . .
I will utter things hidden from of old. . .
we will tell the next generation
the praiseworthy deeds of the Lord,
his power, and the wonders he has done. . . .
so the next generation would know them, . . .
and they in turn would tell their children.
                              (Psalm 78:2–6)

CONTENTS

AUTHOR

Gien Karssen, whose home is in The Netherlands, is the author of *Her Name Is Woman*
(Books One and Two) and *The Best of All*. She
is a Navigator representative in The Hague,
Holland, and has personally ministered to
women throughout Europe for many years.

PREFACE

Possibly nowhere in creation have so many possibilities been left untouched as in the lives of women of all ages. The single woman, living in a society that did not know what to do with her, remained uncertain with regard to her position and opportunities. The question of how she could function fully in society was hardly ever asked. Thus, a lot of creative energy has been wasted.

The idea that God had a purpose for a single woman in his creation was seldom heard. The possibility that certain tasks in society could be performed by her better than by anyone else seemed strange. A woman usually was thought to be intended only for marriage. Yet she proved to be badly prepared for that. Statistics about divorce, the advance of abortion, and the increased addiction to drinking—especially of young housewives—speak for themselves.

I am convinced that God in heaven looked down at all this with grief in his heart, because women did not live up to their potential. The purpose he had in mind for women—married as well as single—was seldom achieved. He thought of the cross that stood in the world 2000 years ago, on which his Son gave his life. That cross did not only prove man's guilt; it also showed his value. By means of that cross God proved that he didn't find the price for saving a woman too high. By means of that cross he showed that he not only wanted to save her for eternity; he also wanted to give her back her lost dignity.

In order not to leave a woman uncertain about all the ambitious plans God had for her, he wrote her a personal letter, a love letter—the Bible. In it every woman can read daily how her life can be meaningful and rich, full of adventure—a feast!

She can learn from the Bible how every day of her life, whether sunny or cloudy, can make its own contribution. If she is open for the things God has to tell her, then she can—with his help—cope with her existence. She will learn from him how to live. She will learn to make the right choices with regard to remaining alone as well as to marriage. But she will learn to say yes to that life and to herself only if she first says yes to God.

The many conversations in this book did take place. Only in cases where it seemed better to me have names been changed.

It is my desire—yes, more than that—my prayer, that *Getting the Most Out of Being Single* may help many women learn how to enjoy the fullness of their lives.

GETTING THE MOST OUT OF BEING SINGLE

1

GOD IS LOOKING OUT FOR YOU

Something happened more than 3,000 years ago that shows how very much God is interested in the single woman. It was a crucial decision that still affects us today!

The Israelites had nearly completed their long migration from Egypt to Canaan and were about to enter the promised land. The land would be precisely divided among the twelve tribes as instructed by Moses. If the leader of a tribe had died during the exodus, his sons, if he had any, were to inherit the land. If there were no sons, the man's brothers would inherit the land.

But something unusual happened at the end

of the exodus. Zelophehad, of the tribe of Manasseh, died in the wilderness. He had only daughters, five of them: Mahlah, Noah, Hoglah, Milcah, and Tirzah. As women they could not lay a claim to the part of the land that should have gone to Zelophehad's offspring. Instead their uncles would inherit the land.

Like thousands of single women before and after them, they felt the burden of their loneliness. God, through Moses, had given clear regulations for women. If a woman was unmarried and still living at home with her parents, her father was responsible for her. If she married, her husband was responsible. But these five daughters, without a father or husbands to care for them, were vulnerable in their society. No one would stand up for them.

They went to the leaders and asked, "Why should our father's name disappear from his clan because he had no son? Give us property among our father's relatives" (Numbers 27:4).

They were honest as they appealed to justice and equity. Because of their manner, their words were evidently convincing. Moses did not reject their plea immediately, as he could well have done on the basis of existing law, but he went to God with their request.

God said, "What Zelophehad's daughters are saying is right. You must certainly give them property as an inheritance among their father's relatives and turn their father's inheritance over to them" (Numbers 27:7).

These five women proved the words of David, to be written many years later: "The Lord is a refuge for the oppressed, a stronghold in times of trouble" (Psalm 9:9). By bringing her difficulties to God, a single woman can avoid self-pity and rebellion, the two dangerous rocks on which the life of the single person most easily runs aground.

Throughout the ages women without fathers or husbands to speak for them have lived with much disappointment and bitterness. But the daughters of Zelophehad showed there was another way. Not only did they get what they asked for, but others shared in their victory. From then on all women of Israel in a similar position would have the rights these five gained. With their brave act, the legal hereditary law of daughters was established.

These five sisters also proved that God doesn't turn a deaf ear to single women. He is concerned with their needs. He loves them and considers their desires, if their motives are pure and their aims acceptable.

A Single Woman Can Work "with" God

A psychologist remarked, "Many girls act as if they think God's arms are too short. I often meet young women who *talk* about God's love, yet it appears to me that very few of them truly experience his love deep in their hearts. They lack the confidence that God is mighty enough to help them in specific situations. Therefore, they go through life afraid and unprotected."

For such women, the story of the daughters of Zelophehad should be encouraging and refreshing. It clearly shows that God's arm is mighty and his hand is strong (Psalm 89:13). His arm is not too short to save; his ear is not unable to hear (Isaiah 59:1).

If a young woman involves God in everything she does and in every circumstance she encounters, she will see him direct her life and make her paths straight (Proverbs 3:6). Then her singleness can prove to be a blessing rather than a hindrance.

With this spiritual attitude, a woman can work *with* God. He can bless other people and achieve new things through such a woman. And her problems will appear in a totally different light. What appeared impossible will change into possibilities through which God can execute his plans—all because a woman was willing to be obedient!

The need of the five daughters to receive their inheritance occurred only once in their lifetime. The people of Israel marched into the promised land only once. The land was divided among the twelve tribes only once. But exactly at that critical moment, the five daughters of Zelophehad acted.

Later, each of the five daughters was married, and with marriage the opportunity to trust God and to be used by him as a single person was gone forever. How sad it would have been if they had missed that chance; sad not only for themselves, but for all the women who have lived after them. Don't miss that once-in-a-lifetime chance that may be decisive for you!

Mahlah, Noah, Hoglah, Milcah, and Tirzah: their names are found only four times in the Bible. But these five sisters have set an example to women everywhere for how to deal with feelings of inequality and oppression. They showed how to behave with dignity in difficult situations. They showed a new way could be found.

It is possible to plead your case in such a way that even God may say, "You are right!"

QUESTIONS FOR STUDY AND APPLICATION

1. Tell the story of these five daughters in your own words.

2. What was the hereditary law in Israel before the five daughters of Zelophehad made their request? What was the big difference afterwards? See also Job 42:15.

3. What description of God, given in Psalm 62:7–8 and 142:4–5, should be a comfort to a single woman? What can she do?

4. According to 2 Chronicles 16:9 and Proverbs 3:5–6, what must a person do to be strengthened and guided by God?

5. In Nehemiah 2 we read the story of a man who had a great concern and responsibility. What principles can you adopt from his approach to the situation?

6. How should a woman see her situation in the light of Romans 2:11 and Galatians 3:28?

7. Did this story change your attitude toward your own circumstances?

Extra study: Write down the names of other women who by courage and tact have greatly influenced history, women from either the Bible or history in general. Are there any in your own surroundings? Who are they and what did they do?

2

GOD HAS A PLAN FOR YOUR LIFE

The temptation of a single woman is to look to the future "for something to happen," while she is missing a life of great adventure and service to God. She may also be lonely and need friendships. Is it all that dismal? Is there no hope?

The single woman can receive solace, for the greatest peace-giving truth can be found in this chapter: *God has a plan for your life*! The Swiss physician Dr. Paul Tournier writes,

> God has a plan for each one of us. He has prepared us for it by means of the particular gifts and temperament he has given to each of us. To discern this plan through seeking day by day to know

9

his will is to find the purpose for our lives. Having an aim in life is a fundamental condition of physical, moral, and spiritual health.[1]

Doesn't it seem reasonable that the God who made each of us so unique that each one's fingerprints are different from those of all other humans could also have a unique plan for our existence? To discover and follow this plan is one of the most fascinating adventures a person can have. We rise above ourselves, for we are involved in a divine plan.

Knowing there is a purpose for our lives, we can live more at peace with ourselves and with the world. We are encouraged to utilize our possibilities to the fullest and be more patient with our shortcomings. We become less upset when everything seems to go against us. In short, we believe that everything we are and have and do fits into the broader perspective of what God is doing with our life.

King David

There is a plan for each individual's existence. The Bible affirms it and gives examples of people who were absolutely convinced of it. David was such a man.

He was deeply convinced that God had been involved even at his beginning.

For you created my inmost being;
    you knit me together in my mother's womb.
I praise you because I am fearfully and wonder-

fully made;
your works are wonderful,
I know that full well.
My frame was not hidden from you
when I was made in the secret place.
When I was woven together in the depths of the
earth,
your eyes saw my unformed body.
All the days ordained for me
were written in your book
before one of them came to be.

(Psalm 139:13–16)

The fact that God was so intensely concerned about every detail of his life amazed
David. It created within him a desire to join in a
teamwork relationship with God, to be totally
obedient to him. David's prayer was, "Search me,
O God, and know my heart; test me and know
my anxious thoughts. See if there is any offen-
sive way in me, and lead me in the way everlasting" (Psalm 139:23–24).

God did search David's heart and point out
things! There were many times in his life when
such correction was badly needed, but the conviction that the purpose of his life was to serve
God never left him. Therefore, he didn't lose
courage about himself. He developed into a man
after God's own heart.

Jeremiah

A decision to live your life totally for God does
not mean you will be without troubles. The

prophet Jeremiah attested to this. He was a man of much sorrow, yet he never doubted that he was called to accomplish a certain mission. The Lord had said to him, "Before I formed you in the womb I knew you, before you were born I set you apart" (Jeremiah 1:5).

Even though Jeremiah felt he was young and incapable, he did God's work. He was to be "a prophet to the nations" (Jeremiah 1:5). A prophet is a man who speaks the word of God on earth—God's messenger or representative. Though it was an exceptional honor, it carried with it certain obligations. For Jeremiah, it resulted in an entire book filled with his lamentations, for the execution of his task was filled with much sorrow.

Paul

Paul was well along in life before his mission became clear to him. For years he had striven after the wrong goal. But from the moment Jesus Christ entered his life, he turned around radically and began living for the purpose for which he was created: "But . . . God, who set me apart from birth, and called me by his grace, was pleased to reveal his Son in me so that I might preach him among the Gentiles" (Galatians 1:15–16).

Paul spent no time looking back at those lost years. Though they had been lived wrongly, they couldn't be undone. Jesus said, "No one who puts his hand to the plow and looks back is fit for service in the kingdom of God" (Luke 9:62).

You and Me

David, Jeremiah, and Paul made their marks on history. They were men who still influence the world today, through God's word. But what about you and me? Isn't it presumptuous to believe that the great and everlasting God has plans for our lives? Aren't we too insignificant for that—too human—too earthly? Yes, without a doubt we are, if we look at ourselves from our point of view. But the Bible advises us not to do that. Instead, it says we must look to God. Then we can see that he has plans for all creation.

Even the animals are part of his grand design. According to Jeremiah 8:7, he has a fixed time for the migration of the stork, the dove, the swift, and the thrush. By instinctively obeying the laws of nature, they do what their Creator expects of them.

Is it plausible that he who plans the flight times and paths of these lower creatures will leave man, the very crown of his creation, in uncertainty about the plan for his life? No, that couldn't be.

Man is endowed with understanding and moral knowledge. There are three ways he can know that God has a plan for his existence: by what he observes in nature; by his inner conscience; and by the words of the Bible itself. Having these three means, all men, of their own free will, can cooperate with God to discover his purposes.

God gave these indicators so that an individual could accept the Person of Jesus Christ, which is the ultimate purpose of every man. He can give no excuse on the day of judgment for not doing so.

What Do People Believe Today?

A young couple printed a Bible verse on their daughter's birth announcement. The words were those God spoke to Jeremiah: "Before I formed you in the womb I knew you."

When asked why they did this, the father explained, "We wanted to express that God was involved with the birth of this new life, as he was involved with our births. This child did not come into existence by accident. God is her creator. I admit, as a human being, I cannot see the full significance of this, especially when I think of the many unwanted children who are born. Yet I am convinced that no life comes into existence without God being part of it. David speaks of this and other Scriptures affirm it.

"My wife and I do not believe, on the basis of these verses, that our daughter is going to have a *special* future. There certainly has to be, in one's unique relationship with God, not only his intention for the person, but also the person's reaction to it. There must be teamwork. But I do believe that God has a definite plan for each person. That, to me, is the biggest difference between Christianity and the other world religions."

Another person who believes the same thing is Widad van der Hoeven, the daughter of Syrian parents, who is married to a Dutchman. She said, "As long as I can remember, I wanted to meet God, but in our home in the Sudan we didn't know him in a personal way. I came to know him through a classmate at a girls' boarding school. She read John 3:16 to me: 'For God so loved the world that he gave his one and only Son, that whoever believes in him shall not perish but have eternal life.' "

So at twelve years of age, Widad asked Christ into her heart. Though very young, she knew at that moment that she should be trained for the service of the Gospel. She explained, "It was as if I heard a voice saying, 'You cannot love me and hate my people (the Jews)!' It was a bitter pill for my Arabian father to swallow when he heard of my double decision."

While in Bible college in Europe, Widad met fellow student Jan Willem van der Hoeven, her husband-to-be and a man who also had a passion for the Jews and Israel. After graduation they devoted themselves to the task of telling Jews and Arabs about Jesus Christ.

The name Widad is classic Arabic and means the same as *agapē*, the Greek word for love used in the New Testament to indicate the deep brotherly and sisterly love among believers. By God's guidance in her life and her teamwork with him in his plans for her, Widad is a demonstration of his abundant love in a city where Jews and Arabs greatly need this love—Jerusalem.

Widad believes that God created every person for a certain task. She says, "We are often blind to it. We do not dare to truly believe it. In order to do so and to trust God in it, a person needs to be freed from himself and from the traditional way of thinking. He has to ask himself, 'What does the Lord mean to me? What do I mean to him?' Though we dare not say, 'If I fail in fulfilling my task, then God will do it with a secondary choice,' I am convinced he will do so."

I, too, believe that God has assigned a task to every man and woman on earth—a task assigned from birth. I believe it is true for me *personally*. What convinces me, in addition to the Bible references, is the story a mother told me many times.

She said, "We were married for some time when the doctor said that I would not be able to have children. We had just lost our first baby in pregnancy. I did become pregnant again, but the same complications occurred as with the first child. I was sure we would lose this baby as well, but my husband believed differently. He said to me, 'I struggled with God for this child and am convinced he will give it to us.'

"The child was born. It was a girl." As the elderly mother said this, she struggled with emotion. She continued, "We experienced this as a miracle of the Lord. We believed that he would lay his hand on this child's life, and that she would grow into a person who would love and serve him."

That mother was right. I am that child.

NOTES
1. Paul Tournier, *The Healing of Persons* (Harper & Row, 1965), pages 260–261.

QUESTIONS FOR STUDY AND APPLICATION

1. Jeremiah 1:5–10 tells of Jeremiah's life purpose.
   What was his task and how far did it reach?
   What was his first reaction to it?
   Who and what made him capable?

2. Galatians 1:15–17 records Paul's vocation.
   Try to describe his task in your own words.
   How did he react to this life purpose?

3. For what task was John the Baptist destined, even from his birth? Read Luke 1:15–17.

4. Who do you think is referred to in Isaiah 49:1, 5–6? What is his purpose?

5. What is the point made by using these illustrations?

6. Do you believe you are personally called by God to accomplish a special task? What is it? What background, experiences, and circumstances point in the direction of your life's purpose? What influence does this study have on it?

Extra study: Read Ephesians 1:1–12. Which people have been set apart for a certain purpose? What is that purpose? When, and on what grounds have they been chosen? What privileges do they enjoy as a result of this?

3

FINDING GOD'S WILL

"Will you do something for me?" How well I remember my sisters asking me that question when I was young. My hesitant answer was, "First tell me what it is!" I was always careful with such a question, for I didn't trust my sisters too much. (For that matter, they didn't trust me, either!) I was always afraid they would ask something impossible of me, so I took no risks.

We all remember doing that from youth, but I wonder if we have truly outgrown that suspicious nature, especially in our relationship with God.

Are You Suspicious of God?

As Christians we know that God is our Father and that he plans what is best for us. We say we agree with Paul when he writes that God's will is good, pleasing, and perfect (Romans 12:2), but to rely upon his will *unreservedly* is quite something else!

Whether we admit it or not, we may actually be afraid that God will hold something back. We might think he doesn't want to give us the very best. Perhaps we worry that he will ask for more than he will give in return. In short, we fear that total surrender to his will means that we will be the loser. Actually, anything less than total surrender means that we will lose a great deal.

God Does Make His Will Known

There are few things as important as knowing God's will for your life. Your usefulness, happiness, and future depend upon it. John says that prayer *makes no sense* if we don't believe that what we ask is in accordance with God's will (1 John 5:14). But can we know what God wants? Isn't it presumptuous to expect such a thing? Isn't it boasting to talk about it?

It would be if God had not clearly expressed himself on the issue. The Old Testament is one continuous record of how God has made his will known to his people. In the New

Testament, Paul told the Ephesians they had to try to understand what the will of the Lord was (Ephesians 5:17). He prayed that the Colossians would know it thoroughly (Colossians 1:9).

"It is not difficult to get to know God's will," says the German author Wilhard Becker. "He helps everyone who shows even the least inclination of wanting to know his will. The difficult thing is to repel one's own will in order to obey the will of God."[1]

Asking God to reveal his will to you means searching and praying for it. This is living by faith. George Mueller of Bristol, England, the well-known foster father of thousands of orphans, became an example of living by faith. He said you may claim to discern God's will only if you are then prepared to obey it.

Nine-tenths of the obstacles to learning God's will are removed if we are prepared to do his will once we learn it, whatever he asks of us. If one is sincerely prepared to obey, it is only a few steps to learning it.

Knowing God's will, then, includes an obligation to do it. Otherwise, it would be analogous to asking for directions from one place to another, but having absolutely no intention of going.

God makes himself known to people who take him seriously. He reveals himself to those who reverently trust him: "The Lord confides in those who fear him; he makes his covenant known to them" (Psalm 25:14). Of course, this intimate relationship with God occurs when you put your faith in Jesus Christ as personal Lord and Savior (John 1:12–13).

Naturally, all of this is true for the Christian single woman. She can arrange her life as she wishes, but she will lose out if she doesn't avail herself of the guidance she has as a child of God. By not obeying him, she isn't allowing him to extend his infinite love to her. She rejects all he has planned to do to make her life successful. By not obeying him she is utterly foolish and shortsighted!

But how can we discover his plan in the confusion and pressure of life? We might envy Adam and Eve who fellowshipped personally with God, or the disciples of Jesus who could talk to him, or even Paul, who upon meeting Jesus on the road to Damascus asked, "What shall I do, Lord" (Acts 22:10).

God is no less approachable for us today. In fact, we can be in touch with him every minute of every day, through prayer. He also wrote a letter in which he recorded all he has to tell us—the Bible.

Many aspects of his will are explicitly revealed in the Bible. For example, we know we should love (Matthew 22:37–39). We also know we should avoid worldliness, greed, and pride (1 John 2:15–16). There are many, many explicit expressions of his will that can be learned by studying the Bible. But many questions in life aren't answered *directly* in the Bible. What do we do then?

Five Ways to Discover God's Will for Your Life

There are five resources we can use to make responsible decisions. They are:

- the Bible
- prayer
- circumstances
- counsel
- personal conviction.

Let's consider these five points in some actual experiences.

Harma was a young woman of thirty who worked in an international Christian organization. She found much fulfillment in her work. One day she met Fred and after some time thought she was falling in love with him. She had to answer the question, Did God bring this man my way, or was it my own doing?

The *Bible* clearly says marriage is an institution of God; therefore, Harma felt no hesitancy to *pray* that God would reveal his will to her in this matter. She claimed promises like Psalm 119:105, in which God said he would lead through his word.

Jeremiah 32:38–39 had particular meaning for her: "I will be their God. I will give them singleness of heart and action, so that they will always fear me for their own good and the good of their children after them." Though God had spoken those words to the people of Israel, they became his specific words to Harma.

The *conviction* developed within her that

God had spoken to her and that she should marry
Fred. She thought of what John had said about
boldness: "And, beloved, if our consciences (our
hearts) do not accuse us—if they do not make
us feel guilty and condemn us—we have confidence (complete assurance and boldness) before God" (1 John 3:21, *The Amplified New
Testament*).

Although this inner certainty plays an important part in knowing God's will, it has to be
handled with the greatest of care because it is
so subjective, especially when considering marriage. The Bible doesn't say in vain that "the heart
is deceitful above all things" (Jeremiah 17:9)! At
no time can the heart be more deceivng than
when a person thinks she is in love.

Harma knew this danger, but she also knew
of God's promise in James 1:5 to give wisdom
to those who ask for it. Because the promises
from God's word seemed to be accumulating and
because as she prayed her inner conviction increased, she decided to seek *counsel* from some
friends who also knew Fred, thus obeying God
in asking advice (Proverbs 12:15). Everyone reacted positively.

But the interesting part of this story is that
the *circumstances* seemed to be absolutely
against marriage. Fred was interested in another girl, and Harma's job took her to another
country. The door appeared completely closed.

All Harma could do was to keep praying and
waiting. After a while, the circumstances of Harma's job changed. In addition, God's Holy Spirit

had been working in Fred's heart, and he asked Harma to become his wife.

As husband and wife, they often help young people find God's will in regard to the choice of a marriage partner. They are sharing with others the principles that worked for them.

Another example comes from my own experience. Some time ago, in planning to write a new book, I intended to visit the Middle East. During visits to Jordan and Israel I planned to have personal conversations with numerous young women. I needed to talk directly with them in order to complete the book. My question was, What is God's will? Should I take the trip or not?

Naturally, the Bible offered no concrete guidance in this case. But that also meant there were no directives against it. In my daily fellowship with God through the Bible, I did read verses that very well could have given encouragement to go.

Prayerfully I made my plans. Everything was developing ideally for me to make the trip until shortly before my departure, when a great restlessness came over me. Initially, I thought it was just nervousness about the complicated journey. But I asked God if I should apply 1 John 3:21. Was the Holy Spirit taking away the boldness and the conviction I had earlier?

I decided to cancel the trip. Within a few days, a number of unexpected circumstances occurred: the outbreak of a contagious epidemic in those countries; the fact that most of the women I was to visit wouldn't be available; and finally, a military escalation in that region. All of these facts, added to my own restlessness and the advice of some counselors not to make the journey, gave me certainty that it was not God's will that I go to the Middle East at that time.

The most important aspect in all of this, according to George Mueller, is our own will. If we subordinate our will to God's will, as Jesus did (Matthew 26:39), then we can trust that God will keep us from the wrong steps. We can believe that he will lead us safely.

No two experiences are the same. Sometimes one of the five resources is stronger than any of the others. But if they are positive, they tell me the same thing that a captain considers before he guides his ship into port. He consults his logbook and navigation instruments and compares them with the data of the coast, the lighthouse, and the harbor lights. When all these agree with each other, he gives the engine room instructions to move forward into port!

With God's will you can move forward confidently, knowing that you are acting according to his plan.

NOTES
   1. Wilhard Becker, *How Should We Pray?* (*Hoe Moeten We Bidden?*) (The Hague: J.N. Voorhoeve, 1974), page 72.

QUESTIONS FOR STUDY AND APPLICATION

1. According to John 4:34, how did Jesus view doing God's will?

2. Read Psalm 40:8.
   a. What did David say about God's will?
   b. On what did he base doing God's will?

3. How do John 4:34 and Psalm 40:8 relate to Romans 12:2?

4. Look up John 14:21. What does God's revelation to us depend upon?

5. What attitude do we need to have in order to discover God's will? Consider Psalm 119:130 and James 1:5.

6. What basic idea do the following verses bring to your mind? Jeremiah 33:3, Matthew 7:7–8, 1 John 5:14

7. List these sources of guidance: the Bible, prayer, circumstances, counsel, and conviction. For each one, describe a situation you experienced in finding God's will.

8. Have you made any wrong decisions that could have been prevented if you had considered the five points above? If so, what? What will you do to prevent this from happening in the future?

9. Is there a decision you must make soon in which you desire that God reveal his will to you? In light of what you know now, how will you make your decision? Be specific with names, facts, dates, and so on.

Extra study: Prayerfully consider Acts 22:14. Check other references for the word *will* in the concordance and write what you learn about God's will.

4

SING, SINGLE WOMAN!

Sing, if you are a lonely woman without a husband? Sing, if you have never known the joy of motherhood? Shout for joy, if you are a widow?

Who can expect that of a single woman? Isn't it contrary to human nature? Living without a husband; never being desired by a man; living your life alone—are not these the things a young woman fears above all else?

Doctors and psychiatrists state that lack of security can create serious problems. Western society, even in the progressive and liberated twentieth century, has little regard for the single woman. In many Eastern countries, she is a despised outcast.

So if a single woman can *accept* being alone, that is a major victory. But can one go even further and claim that being alone is a *source of happiness*? Isaiah, perhaps the best known prophet in the Old Testament, said it can be so: " 'Sing, O barren woman, you who never bore a child; burst into song, shout for joy, you who were never in labor; because more are the children of the desolate woman than of her who has a husband,' says the Lord" (Isaiah 54:1).

But how can a man, even though he is a prophet, make such a statement for a single woman? Does he truly understand what is happening in the mind of a woman? And isn't there a contradiction here, since Eve was told to multiply and bring forth children?

It is natural to ask these questions, but the important thing to remember is that the prophet Isaiah didn't speak on his own authority. It was God himself, through the Holy Spirit, who gave him these remarkable words which open the fifty-fourth chapter. In order to understand more clearly the answers to these questions, we must carefully study the biblical account.

Physical Descendants

God intended man to bring forth descendants to populate the earth. He created the first human couple to begin that task.

Although the Fall tempered the joy of motherhood, a woman continues to experience great happiness from giving birth. She not only enjoys the child, but gets fulfillment from completing the purpose for which she was created. The married woman is envied because of this privilege. It is this moment of fulfillment that separates her from the single woman. Many childless women feel they fall short of true womanhood.

The Old Testament, with its emphasis on the blessings of motherhood, would intensify this feeling, were it not that the original command to populate the earth drew to an end with the coming of the New Testament of Jesus Christ.

Spiritual Descendants

With Christ, the emphasis of man's existence changed. Now, rather than populating the earth, the command is to populate the kingdom of Heaven.

Jesus' appeal to man is spiritual. He shows that the highest aim a man can have is to serve God, for man is first of all a spiritual being. For this reason, Jesus subordinated the husband-wife and parent-child relationships to a relationship with himself. He revealed the temporary character of marriage. It has only an earthly function, for in the future kingdom men and women will not marry (Luke 20:34–35).

Isaiah's call to the unmarried and childless woman must be seen in the light of the coming of Christ. This is evident from the preceding chapter, in which Isaiah announces the coming of the suffering Lord (Isaiah 53:10–11). The purpose of that suffering is offspring; specifically, it is *spiritual descendants*. And this is something in which all people can participate!

Spiritual reproduction was something already revealed in principle to Abraham long before Isaiah prophesied. Not only an earthly nation, but a spiritual nation would descend from Abraham. For this reason he was called "the father of all who believe" (Romans 4:11–12).

Believers would multiply their number by a spiritual process so that the ultimate aim of God—the everlasting meeting of all believers with him in his heavenly home—would be accomplished (John 14:1–3).

Single Women Can Have Spiritual Offspring

Not insignificantly, the *first one* to whom Isaiah announced the joy of having spiritual children was the unmarried, childless woman!

> "Sing, O barren woman,
>   you who never bore a child;
> burst into song, shout for joy,
>   you who were never in labor;
> because more are the children
>   of the desolate woman
> than of her who has a husband," says the Lord.
> "Enlarge the place of your tent,
>   stretch your tent curtains wide,
>   do not hold back;
> lengthen your cords,

strengthen your stakes.
For you will spread out to the right
    and to the left;
        your descendants will dispossess nations
        and settle in their desolate cities.
"Do not be afraid; you will not suffer shame.
    Do not fear disgrace; you will not be humiliated.
You will forget the shame of your youth
    and remember no more the reproach
        of your widowhood.
For your Maker is your husband—
    the Lord Almighty is his name—
the Holy One of Israel is your Redeemer;
    he is called the God of all the earth."

(Isaiah 54:1–5)

Isn't it touching that Isaiah spoke first to the ones with the greatest need of hearing the comforting words?

Through the coming of Jesus Christ a new era arrived for men and women in general, and for single women in particular. From that time on, all women could have a far more meaningful existence than that assigned to them culturally by their society. Any woman—single or married—could have a part in the highest goal ordained to man by God: spiritual descendants.

This privilege of producing spiritual descendants is so closely linked to our relationship with Christ that Isaiah compares it to marriage, as does Paul in 2 Corinthians 11:2—"I promised you to one husband, to Christ."

Isaiah opened up tremendous prospects for the single Christian woman. For the woman of his day, he used the analogy of the goathair tent, the "walls" of the home representing her life. A bedouin tent is a stuffy place. There is no outward view, no perspective. It is confining and suffocating, offering few visible possibilities beyond.

But the coming Messiah changed this. The figurative "walls of the tent" could no longer restrict the woman from having spiritual descendants. The tent pegs would have to be moved outward and the attached cords made longer. In other words, the sphere of her life had to be enlarged.

Therefore, unattached woman, "Sing!"

But what does this mean for a modern, unmarried woman of today? Can it be done? Yes, it can be, and is being done. Joyce Turner is a single American missionary who went to London in 1956 as a staff worker for The Navigators in order to reproduce herself spiritually. Girls she has trained have now gone to all parts of the globe. She has made disciples in many nations and has produced much spiritual fruit.

When asked what the words of Isaiah 54:1 mean to her, Joyce answered, "That someone's value and fruitfulness are not dependent on whether or not she is married. This is a great encouragement, because society still emphasizes the importance of marriage. But the fact that God promises this blessing to a woman, regardless of her marital state, gives single women a very special purpose in life. I have experienced this blessing myself, in ways far greater than I could ever have dreamed."

QUESTIONS FOR STUDY AND APPLICATION

1. Give a definition for the words *fruit* and *fruitful*. Add to those the definitions you find in a dictionary.

2. Using a concordance, look up all the Old Testament references for *fruit* and *fruitful* that refer to having physical children. Briefly, what is said for each reference?

3. Do the same for the New Testament. What do you see?

4. Do the same study again, but this time focus on what the words *fruit* and *fruitful* mean regarding spiritual descendants.
   a. What is the difference between the Old and New Testaments in this respect? In what different ways can a person bear fruit?

5. What did Jesus say about bearing fruit in John 15:1–8 and 16?

6. Answer these questions honestly:
   a. Do I bear fruit?
   b. If so, in which areas do I bear fruit?
   c. Am I multiplying myself in another's life?
   d. In which areas would I like to bear more fruit?

7. Consider John 15:16 in light of this chapter and what you have learned from this study. What can you do in a practical way to start

accomplishing this in your own life? Write the verse on a small card so you can carry it with you all the time.

Extra study: Read through this chapter again, this time giving careful attention to the Scripture references. Write your summary of the subject.

5

DISCOVER YOUR TALENTS
AND USE THEM

You know that God is looking out for you and that you have a purpose for existence. You know you shouldn't wait to give yourself to something that *may* happen in the future. You know also that you can have an endless spiritual ministry by making spiritual descendants.

So what are you going to do with your life? It is imperative for every Christian single woman to learn what her talents are, then begin to use them as her spiritual ministry on earth.

Are You Foolish or Wise?

The story of the ten virgins in Matthew 25:1–13 has profound significance for single women today.

These young women had spent the day helping a bride prepare for her wedding. They bathed her and rubbed her with ointment. They helped her into her wedding dress, putting on her ornaments and pinning on the wedding veil.

When the preparations were completed, all they could do was wait until the bridegroom came with his friends to fetch the bride for the wedding. The marriage celebration, as is the Middle East custom, would take place either in the home of the bridegroom's father or at the home of one of the bridegroom's friends.

For some reason the bridegroom was late. The ten virgins fell asleep. They were awakened at midnight by excited voices outside saying, "Here's the bridegroom! Come out to meet him!"

The bridegroom and his friends were holding small oil lamps. In the dark of the night, one would go out into the streets only with one of these lamps. The virgins needed to take their lamps.

Five of them had taken into account the fact that the bridegroom might be late. They not only had their lamps ready, but had jars of extra oil so they could burn their lamps for the entire celebration. The other five women were unprepared. At this critical moment their oil ran out. They hadn't even brought a small supply of extra oil.

While they rushed about to get some oil, the procession went on its way. All the time and effort they had spent on the preparation for the wedding suddenly proved worthless. When they arrived at the place where the wedding was to be held, the doors were locked. They were too late. Too late forever. Jesus called these girls *foolish*!

The reason this story is so significant is that Jesus is talking about himself. He is the bridegroom. With this parable, Jesus is announcing that he will leave the earth (the absence of the bridegroom while the girls are waiting), but will come back some day, at an unexpected moment (the bridegroom's arrival sometime after midnight). The purpose of the parable is to tell us to stay awake (be prepared), for we do not know the time of Jesus' return.

A person who doesn't take seriously the imminent return of Christ is playing with life. Through their carelessness, the virgins lost their opportunity; they received no second chance.

The same point is made in Jesus' parable of the rich man who went on a long journey (Matthew 25:14–30). He left each of his servants a certain amount of money. When he returned, he asked to see which of the servants had invested it wisely so that each sum would increase. Two of the men multiplied their money. The third man buried it and when the master *unexpectedly* returned, he had nothing to show—absolutely no increase.

The master rewarded the first two men in three ways: they received his praise; they were invited to a feast; and they received further responsibilities.

But the third servant was in trouble. The master said (to paraphrase), "You are a wicked, lazy servant. You could at least have put my money into the bank. Then I would have had some interest. Take the money from this man and give it to the man with the ten thousand gold coins: for to him who uses well what has been given to him, more shall be given. Even the little responsibility given to the unfaithful man shall be taken from him. Nothing can be done with this servant. Throw him out into the utter darkness. There shall be weeping and gnashing of teeth."

We see another example of a person who had spent his time carelessly. He wasted it and was cut off from further and greater responsibilities because every human being is created to *bear fruit*.

The judgment of the five foolish virgins and the lazy servant is similar to the judgment Jesus pronounced on a fig tree that he passed on his way to Jerusalem. When he and the disciples got close, they saw the tree had produced no fruit even though that was the very reason for the fig tree's existence. Jesus said to it, "May you never bear fruit again!" (Matthew 21:18–19).

Live to Bear Fruit

Paul wrote in Philippians 1:22, "If I am to go on living in the body, this will mean fruitful labor for me." He wasn't given fruit. He *labored* for it. For him to live and not bear fruit would have been unthinkable.

Lieutenant Colonel Alida M. Bosshardt of the Salvation Army is one of Holland's best known personalities and a household word in much of inner Amsterdam. She directed the work of the Goodwill Center for thirty years. When she retired recently, she said, "I don't think I could have used my life more fully than I did. And I enjoyed it." Her life of hard work and great toil has produced much fruit, but she also had *joy*. Why? She answered, "Because I have lived through my faith in God. I have been able to practice the gospel. To serve God means to serve people."

Jesus said, "Produce fruit in keeping with repentance" (Matthew 3:8). One's life should be proof of a changed heart. The fruit of the life of Alida Bosshardt is that she passed on the gospel to others. This made her life meaningful. In this way, she gathered fruit for eternal life (John 4:36).

There Are Many Ways to Produce Fruit

Evangelism isn't the only way to produce spiritual fruit. God judges a person by the faithfulness with which she handles what she has received. God has given certain gifts (talents) and abilities to each person. His goal is that we make the best possible use of these talents.

Do you know your gifts? Do you have one, or more than one? You must be able to answer this before you can go on. Often our talents are simply those things that we like to do naturally—things that come rather easily to us. Perhaps some of the following are talents you possess and should share.

Giving money. Paul used the word *fruit* when he wrote about giving money in Philippians 4:17 (KJV). It can be the fruit of your life if you spend it in the service of God.

A seven-year old girl named Judy went to the office of a missionary organization and gave them a dime. "Here you are," she said to the bookkeeper. Not a word more. For a moment, no one understood what she was doing. But one glance at the girl's sweet face made it clear. The bookkeeper realized that Judy had made a great sacrifice. She had just received her weekly allowance and now offered a portion of it to the Lord.

Materially, the ten cents didn't mean much. But spiritually that dime would equal donations of far larger amounts.

Serving. Dorcas, a disciple, produced fruit by using her natural talent of sewing for people in need of clothes (Acts 9:36–43).

Hospitality. Many women in the Bible had the gift of hospitality. This is also true of my friend Conny. She is an educated woman who has traveled extensively, testifying for Christ around the world. "Yet I believe my talent is hospitality," she says. "I know how lovely it is to be received hospitably since I have been in many different homes. It gives me great pleasure to make others comfortable." While talking, she was making a bed—for a guest.

Teaching. My friend Willemien, who is a teacher, discovered that she also has a talent for writing short stories about her class. She does it in an interesting way, always with a spiritual lesson.

Listening. A very special talent all of us can develop is listening. I see this in Caroline. She is forty and has already been bedridden for many years with rheumatism. Statistics show that three out of four patients who are ill over an extended period of time no longer have visitors. With Caroline it is different.

In spite of her illness, her appointment diary is always full. It is, in fact, difficult to get an appointment with her. The secret? It is because she never talks about her pain, though it seldom leaves her. Mostly, she listens. She is truly interested in what other people have to say. Visitors pour their hearts out to her. She gives good advice. Usually, the person visiting her is helped more than she, the patient, is helped.

Speaking. Petra was asked to review a book for a ladies' group. She accepted the challenge, and from that moment on was increasingly in demand as a speaker.

Prepare for Christ's Return

All over the world there is a growing expectation that Jesus—the Bridegroom—will return soon.

Lois, a charming twenty-six-year-old clerk in a fashion boutique, said, "I must tell you that this thought makes me uneasy. When the Lord comes back, what will I have done with my life? What can I offer him? I don't even know what I can do."

So we talked about her starting a discussion group in her home on the subject of women in the Bible. We prepared the first evening's topic together. To help her get started, I led that first meeting.

The group has been meeting for quite some time. Lois handles it very well all by herself now. The women of the group are enthusiastic. Their lives are changing. God's word is influencing them far more than they had ever experienced before. They are developing a vision for others and now save money to help women behind the Iron Curtain. Lois is the most delighted of all of them. She has experienced a joy that she had not expected. *Making use of one's talents for God makes a person happy!*

Jesus has promised that he will return. After his return "we must all appear before the judgment seat of Christ, that each one may receive what is due him for the things done while in the body, whether good or bad" (2 Corinthians 5:10).

It is time for each of us to take personal inventory—to examine our own life, objectively and seriously, lest the Bridegroom be sorrowful about our foolishness and laziness.

QUESTIONS FOR STUDY AND APPLICATION

1. Write your own definitions of the words *talent* and *fruit*.

2. To gain deeper insight on the subject, look up the words in a dictionary and write down the definitions.

3. What does Matthew 7:16–20 teach about bearing fruit?

4. What kind of fruit is mentioned in Isaiah 3:10 and Jeremiah 17:10? In Proverbs 12:14 and Hebrews 13:15?

5. Read Psalm 1:1–3 and Jeremiah 17:7–8.
   a. What conditions for bearing fruit do you discover there?
   b. What kinds of fruit will result?

6. List the talents you have and write beside each one what you have done with it up to now. Ask yourself prayerfully what changes you will have to make in order to utilize them fully.

Extra study: Compare the parable about the rich man in Matthew 25:14–30 with its parallel in Luke 19:11–27. Study them in light of Luke 22:30 and Revelation 2:26 and 22:12. If possible read these portions in several translations.

6

LIVE FOR TODAY

Most single women desire to be married.

That is a continual, underlying dream. This is true even though statistics reveal that the number of marriages in many countries is decreasing and the percentage of divorces is increasing. Statistics don't alter the dreams of the heart!

There is nothing wrong about wishing to marry. Marriage has been established by God, and most women will eventually get married. But it is a negative wish if the desire to marry so dominates her mind that a woman is ineffectual for living in the present. Some tend to think that marriage is the *whole of life*, although it is really only a *part of life*.

Mrs. Dora Winston is the wife of the director of the Belgian Bible Institute. She teaches at the institute, is the mother of grown daughters, and is avidly sought as a speaker. She says, "The girl who doesn't see her wedding day approaching often considers her current existence as only a 'temporary life.' She feels that 'real life' will come later when she marries.

"This is a dangerous way of thinking," Mrs. Winston continues, "because the girl isn't living her present life to its fullest potential. As years go by, this attitude can lead to complaining and frustration. A woman's life may slip through her fingers without her ever realizing it.

"Therefore, my advice to a young single woman is don't consider this period as 'waiting for the best to come.' Women who see marriage as a solution to all their problems will discover that marriage, in itself, gives no total solutions. In fact, married women are often more lonely than singles. And nowhere does the Bible state that being married is a more honorable state than being single."

Taking imaginative flights to a life in the future, instead of enjoying every moment of the present, is a human characteristic. The preschooler longs to go to school. While in school, the student dreams of a career. The young girl wants to be a woman, the woman wants to be a mother, and the mother wants to be a grandmother. Working men and women dream of retirement. We keep preparing ourselves for a life in the future, meanwhile failing to live a full, rich life in the present.

The Cause of This Attitude

English author C.S. Lewis reveals what is behind this mental attitude—or more correctly, *who* is behind it: the devil! Lewis put these words in Satan's mouth in *The Screwtape Letters*: "We want a whole race perpetually in pursuit of the rainbow's end, never honest, nor kind, nor happy *now*, but always using as mere fuel wherewith to heap the alter of the Future every real gift which is offered them in the Present."[1]

Dr. Mette Brolykke, a Danish lawyer who formerly worked in an administrative court for family and marriage affairs in Copenhagen, now has a spiritual ministry among university girls in West Germany. Dr. Brolykke says, "I find that girls often dream their time away thinking about marriage. We young women think too much about the roles of husband/wife, married/single. We compartmentalize our thinking in these categories, rather than concentrating on God.

"Marriage should be seen in the perspective of eternity. This makes it a temporary situation here on earth. Many single women would be far happier if they would judge marriage by what it is—only one aspect of life. It is important, indeed, but it does not encompass all of living. Women must pay attention to the whole of life."

Tomorrow Is Determined by Today

Perhaps it would be helpful to compare one's life to a building, as 1 Corinthians 3:10–13 does. Our life, like a house, is built brick by brick. That which is set down today will be part of the foundation for the bricks of tomorrow, and the day after tomorrow, and so on. What we are able to build in the future is dependent upon what we build today. Each day is important, for each brick is part of the completed building.

The key question a woman must ask is, Am I laying a solid foundation? A girl can begin building her life constructively only if she thinks positively about herself. Feelings of inferiority are rubble that must be cleared away before proper building can begin.

Unfortunately, many sources say a woman is to be taken seriously only if she is married. This helps create feelings of inferiority. But the voices of society shouldn't determine her thinking. Paul states in Romans 12:2 (*Good News for Modern Man*), "Do not conform outwardly to the standards of this world, but let God transform you inwardly by a complete change of your mind." Phillips translates the same verse as, "Don't let the world around you squeeze you into its own mold, but let God remold your minds from within."

Even though society is screaming one thing, a Christian single woman can have a renewed mind as a proper foundation on which to begin building.

What Does God Think?

In Psalm 8:5–6 David acknowledges that God made man "a little lower than the heavenly beings and crowned him with glory and honor." He was made ruler over the works of God's hands; everything was put under his feet. These words should warm a single woman's heart, giving her hope and offering her an amazing task.

Isaiah recorded God's view of man; he is precious, honored, and loved by God (Isaiah 43:4). Jeremiah also quoted the Lord: "I have loved you with an everlasting love" (Jeremiah 31:3). The suffering, death, and resurrection of Jesus Christ shows the extent of the love of God for us. Thus, God's evaluation of a woman has nothing to do with her marital status, but instead with what his Son was willing to give for her—his life!

Develop a New Way of Thinking

If a woman thinks of herself as inferior, therefore, she is doing an injustice to God. She should think, rather, of the way God delights in her, and view each day as an opportunity that is offered only once. Then she won't sacrifice daily opportunities as fuel on the altar of the future or think of being single as an inferior way of living.

This doesn't mean a girl shouldn't be allowed to keep hoping for marriage. But it does mean she should learn to be happy with the life she has, even if it means staying single. She must leave the future to God. He gives the very best to every daughter of his. No one is given his second best. *No one*!

The English mystery writer Agatha Christie writes in her autobiography that few things are more desirable than to be an "accepter" and an "enjoyer." She says if a person puts her mind to it, she can enjoy *everything*, because there is always compensation for what might be missed. For example, you can enjoy the country because of the quiet and the extra time you have for reading or gardening. However, if you live in the city, you can enjoy the advantages of the museums, concerts, and shopping.

The secret of being an enjoyer is *acceptance*; if we accept our circumstances, we can enjoy them. First Thessalonians 5:16–18 says, "Be joyful always ... give thanks in all circumstances, for this is God's will for you in Christ Jesus."

Single women living for a future marriage need a different outlook. However, a new way of thinking won't conquer the problem immediately. There is the continual influence of the media, friends, society, and one's own thoughts. These thoughts must be taken *captive* and submitted to Christ (2 Corinthians 10:5). Only when we truly believe that what God does for us is best, will our lives become enjoyable.

Prayer and the word, together, can help form this foundation of new thinking. And this foundation is the only one that lasts, for it is built on

Christ (1 Corinthians 3:11–12). This is an essential foundation, for if a woman remains single, she will be a more capable worker for God; if she should marry, she will be a much better marriage partner.

The Advantages of Being Single

Nel is a Dutch social worker in charge of assisting discharged prisoners. She doesn't consider her singleness as a temporary, undesirable circumstance, but rather a building block for the remainder of her life. She says, "People often think negatively about being single, but there are advantages as well. You have an opportunity to develop your own personality. If you marry and have children, you may not have time for that." She is right. It is a misunderstanding to think that only marriage gives a woman joy. God intends that women enjoy both spheres of life—singleness and marriage. Each has its specific joys and each has its own problems.

First, the woman should learn to enjoy life and live to the fullest right where she is. To do this, she must have the proper mental attitude. Her main goal must be to give herself totally to God.

"Being single," says Nel, "especially if you are somewhat older, enables one to be more influential than even some married women. This influence is primarily important in the spiritual realm. You have to choose purposely to give yourself to others. This giving of yourself isn't dependent upon whether or not you are married. I want to share with others what I am and what I possess—my whole person. This attitude enriches me as it serves my fellow man."

Serving is hardly a word of this age. You rarely meet a person who uses it, for someone who is serving stops making demands for herself. Such a person is following Christ and is living by grace, and that is an enriching experience.

Servanthood is an attitude of life that lifts *every* person above herself. Jesus said he didn't come to be served, but to serve and to give his life in exchange for the lives of many (Mark 10:45). This attitude gives significance and charm to one's life. It makes one receptive to the surprises God has in store, which he hands out generously to those who have the courage to leave choices to him.

So single women don't have to live in the trap of the future because God himself is their future.

NOTES
   1. C.S. Lewis, *The Screwtape Letters and Screwtape Proposes a Toast* (Time Inc., 1963), page 50.

QUESTIONS FOR STUDY AND APPLICATION

1. Read Romans 12:2 in several translations. What do you think God expects of us?

2. Think about your own life in light of Romans 12:2. Which areas of your thinking need to be changed?

3. Write after each of the following references what the verse means personally to you: Psalm 8:5–6, Isaiah 43:4, and Jeremiah 31:3.

4. Read Jeremiah 29:11 and Psalm 16:11.
   a. On what basis can a Christian have a hopeful expectation of the future?
   b. What conditions, found in Jeremiah 29:12–13 and Psalm 37:4–5, are coupled with those promises?

5. Think about 1 Corinthians 3:10–13, which speaks of building upon the foundation of gold, silver, and precious stones. What could these represent in your life?

6. Tell briefly what you have learned from this study. How are you going to apply what you have learned practically to your life?

Extra study: From the C.S. Lewis quote it is evident that we must take into account the deceptive tactics of Satan. We can resist an enemy only if we know his methods. Therefore, look for answers to these questions: Who is he? What are his tactics? How is he trying to accomplish his ends? How can we resist him? Refer to Luke 4:2, 8:11–12, John 8:44, 2 Corinthians 11:14, James 4:7, 1 Peter 5:8–9, and 1 John 3:8. If you desire to study this subject in more detail, find all the names for Satan in a concordance and study each reference.

7

OVERCOMING LONELINESS

A street reporter for a radio station asked passersby, "Do you ever feel lonely?" Without fail the answer was yes. But what is more striking is that not a single young person said no. Even the youth are lonely.

One young woman said to the interviewer, "I tried to dispel my loneliness at night by drinking, but the next morning the loneliness was back again, as big as ever. Then I became engaged and expected a solution to the problem by being with my fiancé. Nothing was further from the truth. I felt even more lonely than ever. There was no real communication between us, so I broke it off."

There are two important observations about this woman's response. First, she openly admitted she felt lonely. This is positive. One of the problems with loneliness is that we are generally ashamed of it. We can be ill or sad or poor without embarrassment, but for some reason we are ashamed to admit loneliness. However, we come nearer a solution only if we dare face loneliness honestly. We must admit it.

Second, the woman being interviewed made it very clear that *loneliness is not synonymous with being alone*. Many people make that mistake. People jammed together in apartment buildings, supermarkets, and holiday resorts can feel loneliness most acutely.

A young woman said to me, "Visiting mass meetings? Not for me. In such a crowd I feel utterly lonely." I did not expect this of her, for she is young and attractive. She is married, has two children and is well-known in her country.

The Belgian author Phil Bosmans is right when he asserts that loneliness is a moral disease which is not cured simply by putting people together. He writes, "You can be alone, without being lonely. You can be single and feel very safe and happy. And you can be married and together with thousands of people and yet find yourself terribly lonely."[1]

Loneliness Is Universal

A survey was taken among women in The Netherlands asking them to list their basic complaints about life.[2] Thirty-seven percent said they suffered from loneliness. Dr. Jenny de Jong-Gierveld, referring to her doctoral study of three hundred single persons aged thirty to fifty-five, said that more single men expressed loneliness than single women. Her report also revealed that marriage is no safeguard for loneliness. No less than twenty-seven percent of the married women indicated they felt very lonely. (Among single women it was thirty-two percent.)[3]

Numbers only confirm that loneliness isn't restricted to a certain age or group. There are few people on earth who are unable to sympathize with David when he complained, "I am lonely and afflicted" (Psalm 25:16).

David, that great man of God, was lonely.

Prince Hendrick of The Netherlands expressed acute loneliness. He had chiseled these words on his dog's gravestone: "Could one have friendship with animals, then here lies my truest friend indeed."

But perhaps the loneliest of all men was Jesus. He went through a loneliness so deep we cannot possibly understand it. His loneliness began with his incarnation: Paul describes that Jesus "made himself nothing" by taking on human likeness (Philippians 2:7–10).

It appeared that no human soul understood him while he was on earth. He was lonely in the circle of his earthly family because his own brothers didn't believe in him (John 7:3–5). He remained single. He was deserted and misunderstood by his own people, the Jews, who didn't comprehend his mission (John 6:15).

He was lonely even among his disciples. They left him in his hour of deepest distress. Even his intimate friends among the disciples failed him. They weren't able to watch with him for even a single hour (Matthew 26:36–45). The loneliest moment of his earthly life came on the cross, when he cried out, "My God, my God, why have you forsaken me?" (Matthew 27:46). That made his loneliness complete.

The Origin of Loneliness

God, who knows us through and through because he created us, knew we needed someone with whom we could share our life. He said, "It is not good for the man to be alone. I will make a helper suitable for him" (Genesis 2:18). He then created Eve.

To her honor, she filled the missing link in God's creation. Her task was to abolish the loneliness of the first man on earth. She did this very well initially, while her relationship with God was intact. It was God's intention that these harmonious relationships of human-to-God and human-to-human continue forever.

But sin entered the world when Eve disobeyed God and drew Adam into the sin. They became sinful and lonely people at the same time. People who lose God also lose each other. The man and woman, who were created to express the greatest possible union between two people in marriage, experienced a disintegrating element that penetrated their union, a disintegration that would spread itself on and on through future generations (Genesis 3:12–15).

Adam and Eve were not alone, for they still had one another. Yet, inwardly, they became strangers to one another. Their relationship was ruptured. Instead of protecting and supporting each other, they deserted one another. Their union was broken. With that break, their personal loneliness became a fact.

And the life of every human being has been permeated with loneliness ever since—even the life of Christ. But his loneliness was not without meaning, for it was meant to bring people back to God.

The gap between God and man, which came into existence because of Adam and Eve, was bridged by Christ. Spiritual loneliness—being out of touch with God—was abolished by Christ. He opened a way back to God through belief in himself as Savior. For people who accept Christ as their personal Lord and Savior, loneliness becomes relative. Although loneliness still remains part of our human existence, no person needs to be forsaken by God any longer.

In fact, the lonely person—the lonely single woman—can remove much of her loneliness. She can also personally become the means through which other people become less lonely.

How to Overcome Loneliness

Here are five ways to overcome loneliness (and this is by no means an exhaustive list).

Admit Your Loneliness

Jesus did not disguise it; we should not disguise it. We must not be embarrassed to seek the help of others. Jesus was not ashamed to share with others the deepest loneliness of his life. When he went to the cross, he allowed his friends to know he was in trouble and that he appreciated their sympathy and help: "My soul is overwhelmed with sorrow to the point of death. Stay here and keep watch" (Mark 14:34).

What keeps us from allowing others to share in our lonely distress? Pride? False shame? Self-protection? Or simply a lack of friends to resort to when our spirits are low?

I discussed this with Stephany, a mother of three young children, who is married to a man whose work often takes him away from home for weeks at a time. She said, "You must have very good friends indeed to be prepared to put yourself into such a vulnerable position. Sometimes when you share your misery you receive a cold shoulder. I believe I can only go to another Christian for true comfort."

She is right. When two people allow each other to express their inner feelings, it is amazing how much kindness results. All it takes to start is humility. Be willing to take the weaker position. Simply let the other know that you want help.

Use Spiritual Means

In the Bible we read of Jesus and others and how they handled times of loneliness and sorrow. Jesus, who went through loneliness like no other, truly understands us. He invites us to depend on him for help (Hebrews 4:15–16). By the word and prayer we can live a God-centered life. A person who lives in this manner can overcome a great deal of loneliness.

In one respect, loneliness can be compared with salt. Salt is a taste-giving ingredient, a useful element for meals. But it also produces thirst. What salt does for our food, loneliness can do for our life—make us thirsty for God. Because of our relationship with God, we can empathize with the loneliness of others, thus helping and serving them in their unhappiness. This, too, takes us out of ourselves.

Involve Another Person

My good friend Tine died last year. I have her birthdate written in my diary. When that day came this year, I had planned to call her husband, Dave, to console him. But before I had a chance to do so, he called me!

"Today you are also having a sad day," he said. "I just wanted you to know that I empathize with you. I have just phoned Tine's mother and sister as well." He was a man who could expect others to help soften his loneliness. Instead, he thought of others first—those who were, to a lesser degree, affected by the same sorrow. Thus the sad anniversary of Tine's birth became a day of special radiance for everyone concerned because David was wise enough to involve others. Second Corinthians 1:3–4 refers to "the God of all comfort, who comforts us in all our troubles, so that we can comfort those in any trouble with the comfort we ourselves have received from God."

Become a Good Listener

A good talk with another person can work wonders, especially if we have learned to listen really well. By listening carefully, we are telling the other person that we are sincerely interested in him. We are saying we find him worthwhile.

It is surprising how much less lonely we would be if we could learn to listen more and better. There are people (unfortunately, many women among them) who condemn themselves to deep loneliness simply because they talk on and on endlessly. By talking constantly they estrange others, and at the same time gain no new viewpoints on life.

Ask good questions to get others to talk. Then LISTEN! Often in a group we torture ourselves wondering what we should say, when actually the other person only wants you to listen. She needs a person with whom she can express her deeper self. She would open up through questions initiated by your true interest.

Once I was invited to a dinner with some diplomats and their wives. After my first real feminine problem was solved (what I should wear), I panicked. What on earth could I talk about? How could I make a sensible conversation in a foreign language, especially about politics, a field in which I feel very ill at ease?

But when I sat next to a senior official, I regarded him first as a person, second as a diplomat. This led me to ask him about the things that interested him as a human being: his impression of our country; his experiences with a foreign language; how his wife and children were becoming accustomed to Holland; where his previous post was. They were simple questions on a human level. From his avid reaction I realized he was more interested in talking about these things than international affairs, for he had to do that officially all day long.

Later, the hostess told me that this gentleman had enjoyed the evening tremendously. And I had greatly enjoyed myself as well. The moment I had been afraid of, namely that I would be crippled in conversation, did not even occur. I not only had a pleasant evening, but I learned things from him that I could not have learned anywhere else.

Become Interested in Others

I know of an X-ray technician who was so uncertain of herself in a group that she always drank several glasses of wine before going out. This gave her courage. But when she arrived at the gathering, she had to quickly renew her courage by drinking more wine before she finally dared to talk a little.

One day she met a colleague who was a Christian. This new friend invited her to a Bible study group. She saw that she was accepted in this group. Her trust in God and people began to grow. Eventually, the cork stayed on the wine bottle when she had to meet new people. Finally, she came to believe in God. She learned to express herself. Many beautiful traits and strengths of character became visible that were earlier veiled by loneliness.

Now nobody recognizes her as the frustrated girl of the past. "I cannot imagine that she has *ever* been lonely," said one friend who now knows her very well.

The X-ray technician not only focused on God, but she became aware of others around her. Instead of concentrating on herself and her problems, she began to get interested in others. Instead of demanding attention, she learned to give it.

A person who, because of her relationship with God, lives for others is like salt in society. She adds taste and zest to life again.

Realize Your Value
A friend of mine who is a nurse said, "If I feel lonely, I do several things. First, I try to tell someone else what it is that is bothering me. That gives quick relief. Then I simply go on with the work I need to do. I no longer have self-pity for my low spirits.

"I also realize my own value, for as a human being I have so many possibilities. I don't think of myself as unimportant. God finds me important. I think of Jesus' words: 'If anyone loves me, he will obey my teaching. My Father will love him, and we will come to him and make our home with him' (John 14:23). Yes, *I am important* for the Savior and the Creator of the universe to do that with me!"

Loneliness, seen in this light, can be dealt with and defeated.

NOTES

1. Phil Bosmans, *My Dear I Love You!* (*Menslief Ik Hou Van Je!*) (Amsterdam: Lannoo Tielt, 1976), page 79.
2. "Woman '78" ("Vrouw '78"), an investigation of women in The Netherlands, by Novum B.V. and IPM (daily paper *Trouw/Kwartet*) August 31, 1978, page 5.
3. Jenny de Jong-Gierveld, *Singles* (*Ongehuwden*) (The Netherlands: Samsom N.V., Alphen aan de Rijn, 1969).

QUESTIONS FOR STUDY AND APPLICATION

1. Look up the word *loneliness* in a dictionary. Think about the definition and add to it if you can.

2. Read the story of Jesus and the Samaritan woman in John 4. Why do you think she was a lonely woman?

3. Study the conversation between Jesus and the Samaritan woman from the point of view of the technique that Jesus used.
   a. Write down all the points that attract your attention. For instance, in verse seven he began the conversation with a *request*.
   b. Did Jesus work toward a certain culmination in the conversation? If so, what was this point, and was it achieved?

4. Do you believe the woman was less lonely after the meeting with Jesus? On what do you base your answer?

5. Jesus said in Matthew 5:13, "You are the salt of the earth." How do you see this being expressed in the life of the Samaritan woman?

6. What have you learned about your own loneliness? What is the place a conversation can have in loneliness? What are you going to do about your loneliness—and the loneliness of others—as a result of reading this chapter?

Extra study: Examine the conversation technique used by Jesus again. Outline it briefly so you can use it as easily in your own conversations.

8

THE UNIVERSAL NEED FOR FRIENDSHIPS

"I am privileged," the man said during a television interview. "I haven't lived in vain, for I have had at least one real friend in my life. Not many people can say that."

The speaker was a well-known athlete. In reviewing his life and accomplishments, his main impression was not his achievements in sports, but the memory of that one friend who made life worthwhile for him.

An elderly friend, who knew her day of widowhood was approaching, prayed to God for a good friend. He heard her prayer. Because she learned to focus on friendship, she wasn't as lonely when her husband died as she would have been without that focus.

People who pray for friendships must be prepared to receive them from God as a very special surprise. That is the case with Marianne and Hilde. Each one wanted to deepen her spiritual life. In prayer they asked the Lord for another with whom to experience this. God brought them together one day in a casual meeting. This developed into a deep friendship. They now have a bi-weekly get-together, during which they share experiences, pray, and study the Bible. They pray for others, especially for friends who are working in lonely places around the world.

The need for friendship is univeral. Everyone needs a friend who, as Solomon says, "loves at all times" (Proverbs 17:17). We all desire someone to love us for who we are, with all our frailties and weaknesses, not just for what we do or possess. It is not remarkable that the Bible says a great deal about friendship (there are almost one hundred verses on this subject).

Single Women and Friendship

It is an interesting fact that the magnificent Bible stories about friendships all involve men. Is this due to the fact that we meet more men than women in the Bible? Or is it a commentary on women? Are we women more hesitant in forming real relationships? Are we possibly more shallow in our devotion and loyalty to each other than men are? Or do we feel more vulnerable in our relationships because our feelings are more easily involved? Are we afraid we will be hurt?

It may be that a single woman fears that her chances for marriage will diminish if she gives herself in true friendship to another woman. I believe the opposite is true. Friendship might be the very best preparation you can have for marriage, because it helps develop us into multi-faceted personalities.

Great Friendships in the Bible

Because having friends is a universal need, I think it is important that we explore the whole area of friendships.

Job

One of the oldest stories of true friendship was told about Job. He was stripped of everything. His children were dead. His possessions were lost. His health was broken. His wife did not support him.

Job experienced the truth expressed by Solomon in Proverbs 18:24—"There is a friend who sticks closer than a brother." His friends remained faithful to him during his time of greatest need. Their own needs and interests receded into the background when they heard of Job's misery. They agreed to go to Job to comfort him. (It is interesting that we didn't learn that

Job had brothers and sisters until his former prosperity was restored.)

When his friends first confronted Job, they saw that his sorrow was too great for words. A respectful silence was appropriate, so they sat with him for seven days and seven nights without saying a word. Job not only had friends, but friends who knew to keep silent when there was nothing yet to say.

One of the blessings of true friendship is that we can be honest. We need not pretend to be better than we are or something other than what we are. When Job felt that even God had deserted him, he didn't hesitate to share this with his friends: "Have pity on me, my friends, have pity, for the hand of God has struck me" (Job 19:21).

Friendship is dependent on interaction. All good friendships are a matter of give and take. There is joy and pain. Even the best of friends disappoint us now and again. It is because they are human. So in the final analysis, we must resort to God, not to friends. When Job's friends disappointed him, he cried out to God (Job 16:20).

At one point, Job's friends needed *him* to invoke God's forgiveness for *their* shortcomings. "I am angry with you. . . ." God said to the three, "because you have not spoken of me what is right, as my servant Job has. . . . My servant Job will pray for you, and I will accept his prayer and not deal with you according to your folly" (Job 42:7–9).

There is an important spiritual relationship

between expressing friendship and one's fear of God. "He who withholds kindness from a friend forsakes the fear of the Almighty" (Job 6:14, *Revised Standard Version*).

David and Jonathan

The most moving biblical story of friendship is that of David and Jonathan (1 Samuel 18:1–4, 19:1–7, and 20). These two men could easily have been fierce opponents, for one was the son of the ruling king, and the other was the appointed successor to the king. Instead of being separated by jealousy, the two were united by a deep and growing affection.

This attachment was so great that each loved the other more than his own self. This is the highest level of friendship. It remains faithful until death. In fact, it went beyond death in this case, for David showed favor to Jonathan's son after Jonathan's death (2 Samuel 9).

Their mutual affection was rooted in God. Together, they had made an alliance with God.

Jesus

As a human being, Jesus obviously needed friendships. He had friendly associations with his disciples and an intimate friendship with Lazarus (John 11:11). He also enjoyed warm friendships with Lazarus's sisters, Martha and Mary. He regularly visited their home.

The highest peak of friendship for Jesus was most likely experienced with three of his disciples on the mountain of transfiguration (Matthew 17:1–9). The lowest point was when his friends deserted him in the darkest hour of his life (Matthew 26:26–46).

All people need one intimate deep friendship. Jesus had this in John, the disciple whom he loved above all others (John 13:23).

How to Nurture Friendships

How do friendships evolve? How are they nurtured? According to Proverbs 18:24 (KJV), "A man that hath friends must shew himself friendly."

Friendship is like a plant that grows slowly and needs continuous care. Friendship costs time and effort. A person who wants to experience friendship has to first be a good friend himself. If we are not willing to do this, we cannot expect to make friends. Here are some practical tips.

Think of the Other Person

I will always remember a day when I returned from a vacation to my apartment, where I live alone. I had been abroad, amid the people and sights and sounds of an exciting country. It had been a delightful time. As I entered the quiet of my apartment, there was somewhat of a letdown. But soon the phone rang. It was my friend Yolanda. She said, "I'm just calling now for it is a time like this when a woman needs to talk. Tell me what you did. Tell me all about your holiday."

The conversation took no more than fifteen minutes, but for me it was an expression of true, thoughtful friendship. It was so appreciated because it came at precisely the right moment!

Give Quality Time

I overheard a woman say to her friend, "I admire the way you give yourself to me as if I were the only person in the world in whom you are interested." The other woman answered, "That is true. At this moment there is nobody more important to me than you."

Communicate

One of the greatest causes of failure in marriage is lack of communication. Many fail in communicaton because they didn't learn to open up to another person *before* they were married. This is why it is so important for single women to learn to give of themselves to others before marriage.

Communication is not only giving, it is listening. It is a give-and-take situation. "As iron sharpens iron, so one man sharpens another" (Proverbs 27:17).

Serve

The richness of friendship lies in willingness to give of one's self. Friends must not be used or taken advantage of; they are to be served. Friendship costs something. It never presents itself as a rose without thorns. Those who shun thorns must not pick roses. But then think how colorless life would be!

Give Constructive Criticism

It is difficult for anyone to take criticism from someone else. Our pride resists this to the end. But Solomon, in his wisdom, wanted criticism. He said that he preferred the faithful wounds of a friend above the kisses of an enemy (Proverbs 27:6).

Real friends can be God's instruments through which we can grow. We must learn to give and accept criticism in love.

Friendship in Marriage

Friendship with one's spouse is indispensable for the married person. A strong friendship should be the starting point in the love relationship. The two do become one. No wonder the bride in the love song of Solomon says of her bridegroom, "This is my lover, this is my friend" (Song of Songs 5:16). For her, the words *lover* and *friend* mean the same person.

But the married couple must also have other friends. Her husband takes first place, of course, but the wife should maintain contact with her friends and continually develop new relationships. This will enrich her life. She will need these friends when her husband travels or when she is left home all day with no one to talk to but small children.

Perhaps this little poem by Dinah Maria Mulock Craig best sums up what true friendship is.

FRIENDSHIP

Oh, the comfort—the inexpressible comfort
    of feeling safe with a person.
Having neither to weigh thoughts,
Nor measure words—but pouring them
All right out—just as they are—
Chaff and grain together—
Certain that a faithful hand will
Take and sift them—
Keep what is worth keeping—
And with the breath of kindness
Blow the rest away.[1]

NOTES

1. Dinah Maria Mulock Craig, in *Friendship*, compiled
    by Ralph L. Woods (Norwalk, Connecticut: C.R.
    Gibson Publishers, 1969), page 10.

QUESTIONS FOR STUDY AND APPLICATION

1. Which characteristics of friendship are mentioned in Proverbs 17:7 and 27:6, and Luke 11:5–8 and 15:6–9?

2. Read Acts 27:3. What did friends mean for Paul when he was a prisoner?

3. Read the story in Acts 10:24–28. What did Cornelius think was important for his best friends?

4. What are some key teachings regarding friendship that we must put into practice? Refer to Proverbs 16:28, 17:9, and 27:10.

5. What conclusions do you draw about friendships after reading Exodus 33:11, Isaiah 41:8, and James 2:23?

6. What did Jesus say about friendship in John 15:13–15?

7. What are you going to do to strengthen friendship in your own life?

9

WHAT THE BIBLE SAYS ABOUT WORK

The first way in which God revealed himself to us is as a God who *works*: "In the beginning God created the heavens and the earth" (Genesis 1:1). In Genesis 1:26–28, we see the origin of work for man.

> "Let us make man in our image, in our likeness, and let them rule. . . ." So God created man in his own image, in the image of God he created him; male and female he created them. God blessed them and said to them, "Be fruitful and increase in number; fill the earth and subdue it. Rule over the fish of the sea and the birds of

the air and over every living creature that moves on the ground."

The significance of these words is often lost on us when we casually read the Genesis account. It means, however, that we are responsible for the entire creation which God has spread before us, not only for the physical environment of nature, but for all spiritual and moral life as well.

In this task, man and woman originally stood beside each other as equals in their responsibility toward God. Unfortunately, the balance here, as in many other instances, has been disturbed by the Fall. For all sorts of reasons, woman has lagged far behind in the execution of her part in that task.

This could originate from an incorrect interpretation of Genesis 3:15–19, where we read that the woman will feel the consequences of sin *particularly in the area of motherhood*. The man experiences the consequences in the sphere of his daily work. But nowhere does the Bible state that from the Fall onward man alone is totally responsible for the world and society, while the woman is responsible solely for the family.

Dora Winston says, "The Bible takes the father duties of the man seriously, so he cannot say to his wife, 'The children are your business; do what you like, but leave me alone.' This is often thought and practiced, even if it is not said. On the other hand, a woman is more than the sum total of her biological functions. During her entire adult life she cannot restrict herself to the home by giving the excuse, 'We live in a man's world.' "

Woman was also told to subdue the earth and to have dominion over the entire realm of nature. This is a command in the broadest terms, covering the sciences, research, production, medicine, welfare, education, politics, business, government, art, literature, and all other aspects of our existence.

Mrs. DeBacker, the Belgian Minister of Cultural Affairs, could have been paraphrasing Genesis 1:28–29 when she said, "It is unthinkable to restrict the interest of the woman to the so-called 'feminine sectors.' The education of children is too important to leave only to women. The edification of society is too important to leave only to men."

Work in the Bible

The word *work* and its derivations occur some hundred times in the Bible. Working is a biblical concept: "Six days do your work" (Exodus 23:12). God gave work not only because it provides a way to meet our physical needs, but because working meets an inner human need. To work is to experience satisfaction and joy. In Genesis 1:31, we read that God gained satisfaction from his work.

One of the things that makes the woman in Proverbs 31 so attractive is that she obviously derives pleasure from everything she does: "She . . . works with eager hands" (Proverbs 31:13).

Work was a normal experience for Jesus. He said, "My Father is always at his work to this very day, and I, too, am working" (John 5:17). For Jesus, performing his task was a necessity of life, like eating and drinking. "My food is to do the will of him who sent me and to finish his work" (John 4:34).

Just before his death Jesus said, "I have brought you glory on earth by completing the work you gave me to do" (John 17:4).

Paul wrote, "Whatever you do, work at it with all your heart, as working for the Lord, not for men, since you know that you will receive an inheritance from the Lord as a reward. It is the Lord Christ you are serving" (Colossians 3:23–24).

These biblical statements elevate every kind of work to the highest level. There really is no difference between what people call "important" or "less important" work. The only important difference is with what attitude we do it. All work is service rendered to God. If we can actually remember we are *working for him*, then work becomes a part of eternity.

Women at Work in the Bible

The Bible has many accounts of women fulfilling responsibilities in many walks of life: Deborah (Judges 4 and 5) and Huldah (2 Chronicles

34 and 35) both had governmental and spiritual influence; the midwives Shiphrah and Puah (Exodus 1:15–21) used their knowledge and devotion to assure the survival of the Jewish people; women served as queens (1 Kings 10:1–12 and Acts 8:27), a female political consultant (2 Samuel 20:16–22), artists and craftsmen (Exodus 35:25–26), and musicians (Exodus 15:12 and 1 Chronicles 25:5–6).

Nowhere does God disapprove of these women and their work. To the contrary, they all have their place in the total fabric of biblical history. Some women were married, some were single. In fact, the Bible's portrait of the ideal woman in Proverbs 31 is that of a woman who combines motherhood with her profession. God obviously approves of a woman who works!

QUESTIONS FOR STUDY AND APPLICATION

1. Read Genesis 1. What do you find there about the work of God?

2. Study the following verses about Jesus' view of work and write a summary: John 4:34, 6:27, 9:4, and 17:4.

3. Read Exodus 1:15–22. What strikes you about the task of the midwives Shiphrah and Puah? Before you answer, put yourself in their place. What was at stake? What was their deepest motive in their work and what were the consequences of it?

4. Deborah (Judges 4 and 5) and Huldah (2 Chronicles 34 and 35) worked with men. What principles can we learn from them?

5. The queen of Sheba was a woman of power and respect (1 Kings 10:1–13). What strikes you about her? Why did she want to personally get acquainted with Solomon? What was she willing to give in order to do this? What were the consequences?

6. Summarize what you have learned about work. How will this affect your attitude toward working?

Extra study: Look up the word *work* and all its derivatives in a concordance and do a study on the subject. List other people in the Bible who are examples of working women.

10

WOMEN AT WORK

Dr. Clyde M. Narramore, founder and director of the Narramore Christian Foundation, writes in his book *How to Choose Your Life's Work*,

> We see numerous young women who come for counseling. Many have married shortly after leaving school. These women come to our clinics feeling discouraged, depressed, frustrated, and confused. Many of them seem to have lost their identity. They are frustrated with cooking, cleaning, and changing children's clothes. "I just want to have fun," they will say. "I've had all I can take. I've always wanted to be a person, but I

just feel that I'm a cog in a machine. I can never be myself."

One of the most significant times of life is the late teens and early twenties. If a person is single, she can assume a measure of independence, develop her interests, travel, and in many other ways grow into a happy, well-adjusted person. But many girls skip this important time of life. They go directly from their teen years into marriage and for many years unknowingly search for this time of growing up and becoming a satisfied young adult. Now their marriage reflects this serious lack.

On the other hand, many girls, after completing high school or college, obtain employment. Becoming individuals, they enjoy their young adult years. They handle their own finances. They travel. For the first time they are not dependent upon their parents; they function as grown-ups. After two or three years of single adulthood, these girls are better prepared for the responsibilities of marriage. The whole demeanor of these women is raised to a new level because they were able to take a few years after school to develop on their own without the responsibilities of married life.[1]

When we look at the task given in creation—the edification and maintenance of society—it is obvious that this cannot be executed by married women only. Single women are *essential* to fulfill certain tasks for which they are uniquely qualified and to which they feel called.

Think of what Mother Teresa, recent recipient of the Nobel Peace prize, means for thousands of starving people in India. Consider women like Florence Nightingale, Henrietta Mears, Evangeline Booth, and Corrie ten Boom. This doesn't mean there is a place only for the exceptionally talented woman. Every woman has the privilege and duty to make a contribution to society.

Christian Women Talk About Working

On one occasion I met with about twenty Christian working women. Most of them were single. We discussed what it is like being a Christian woman working in the marketplace. Here are just a few guidelines developed from the discussion.

Be obedient. Astrid, a thirty-seven-year-old analyst, said, "Doing what is asked of me by my boss is a biblical order I obey." This is a surprising statement in a time when employees talk of little else but equal rights. Yet Astrid is correct, for Ephesians 6:5 teaches, "Obey your earthly masters with respect and fear, and with sincerity of heart, just as you would obey Christ."

Romans 13:1–2 teaches,

> Everyone must submit himself to the governing authorities, for there is no authority except that which God has established. The authorities that exist have been established by God. Consequently, he who rebels against the authority is

> rebelling against what God has instituted, and those who do so will bring judgment on themselves.

This is not meant to be a restriction, but to insure our protection and enrichment.

Astrid continued, "This doesn't mean that I don't take initiatives. I often do and it is appreciated very much."

Wilma, a secretary, said, "Obeying, yes. But only if it doesn't interfere with God's commandments. The other day my boss asked me to tell a customer that he wasn't there. I refused. I couldn't reconcile it with my conscience. I also felt he was not entitled to ask me to do this. Telling lies was not included in my job description."

Wilma is correct. The Bible teaches that we must obey God rather than men (Acts 5:29). This was the only choice for Wilma, for God said we should not lie to one another (Colossians 3:9), but rather speak truthfully to our neighbor (Ephesians 4:25).

God often rewards such faith in his word. In Wilma's situation, her boss apologized and asked why she had done this. She was able to tell him about Jesus Christ, accounting for her faith in a proper way (1 Peter 3:15).

Have a positive attitude. One girl said, "At work I apply being a Christian by having a positive attitude. If people talk negatively about a colleague, I do not take part in it. I try to counterbalance by telling something positive about that person."

Be honest. Another woman in the group said, "I try not to make myself look better than

I am. I try to have the courage to admit my weaknesses. Christians often want to appear perfect, I think. If we make mistakes, why should we hesitate to admit them? My security doesn't depend upon what my colleagues think of me, but on how God judges me."

Involve God in problems. Hilda told how a particular situation frustrated her. "The tensions came to a head one morning when we had a staff meeting. I was fearful that the younger male colleagues wouldn't understand the matter that was bothering me and would make a wrong decision. That morning in my quiet time, I meditated on Philippians 4:6–7—'Do not be anxious about anything, but in everything, by prayer and petition, with thanksgiving, present your requests to God. And the peace of God, which transcends all understanding, will guard your hearts and minds in Christ Jesus.'

"Because the younger men were responsible, I had been hesitant to voice my opinion. But I put all my anxieties before the Lord in my quiet time. The staff meeting went smoothly. It was unbelievable the difference that verse made! The difficulties solved themselves without my intervention. It was a marvelous experience to know that you can involve God in your work in such a practical way."

Set your priorities. The professional life takes up much of a woman's time. It is essential to set your priorities early in your career planning, so you will have balance between your working life and your spiritual ministry.

One nurse said, "I have purposely given up promotion. If I accept it, I will have little time left to give myself to people. I want to remain available to help other women in their Christian life. I want to show them what Christ means to me and what he can be to them. That is the most important thing to me."

Another woman added, "I would love to become a veterinary surgeon. My education would qualify me to do it. But I know if I choose that profession, I will not have time for anything else. Therefore, I'm looking for a less demanding job. The remaining time I'm going to spend on what Jesus told us to do in Matthew 28:19— 'Make disciples.' "

NOTES
1. Clyde M. Narramore, *How to Choose Your Life's Work* (Zondervan Publishing House, 1977), pages 12–13.

QUESTIONS FOR STUDY AND APPLICATION

1. Study Exodus 20:9, Ephesians 4:28, and 2 Thessalonians 3:10. What are some biblical reasons for working?

2. What attitude characterized the work of people in the following verses? Nehemiah 4:6, 6:3–9, Proverbs 31:13, and 1 Thessalonians 2:9

3. What advice does the Bible give in regard to this subject in John 6:27 and Colossians 3:17?

4. What warning do we read in Proverbs 6:6, 10:4, and 21:25?

5. What blessings from God do Deuteronomy 15:10–11, Haggai 2:4, and 1 Corinthians 3:13–14 promise?

6. Write a brief application for yourself regarding what you have learned about work. Memorize Proverbs 3:5–6.

Extra study: Read the entire book of Proverbs and underline everything you find applicable to work. Chapters six, ten, twelve, nineteen, and twenty especially give practical advice.

11

SO YOU WANT TO BE A MISSIONARY

Dawson Trotman, founder and first president of The Navigators, told of an experience he had as a member of a committee considering the applications of twenty-nine young mission candidates. Each of the young people had completed his studies at either a university, Bible school, or seminary. Two of the numerous questions Trotman asked each of the candidates were extremely revealing.

The first had to do with their personal spiritual life. "How is your daily relationship with God; do you feel your relationship with him is as he wants it to be?" From that select group of people, *only one* felt that his spiritual life was as it should be.

Dawson's second question was, "How many people can you call by name who were won by you for Christ and are still living for him at this moment?" He prefaced the question with comments about how each of them obviously desired to go overseas to win men and women to Christ, and then have those new converts go out into their own society to win still others. Most of the candidates had to admit that *they yet had to win one person to Christ*. They were woefully unprepared to become missionaries, which was Trotman's point.

There are no part-time Christians. If we can't be missionaries right at home, we won't be missionaries in another country where there will be a multitude of other problems and pressures. You can—and must—do God's work right where you live.

The Challenge: "Go into All the World"

There are some people who want to make the work of the church, missions, or a Christian organization their lifetime occupation. Some give their lives to answer Christ's call for workers: "Ask the Lord of the harvest, therefore, to send out workers into his harvest field" (Matthew 9:37–38). They are "called" by him to perform a certain task. They go into the world to proclaim the gospel, the good news that there is redemption in Jesus Christ.

Paul felt called to proclaim the gospel: "Paul, a servant of Christ Jesus, called to be an apostle and set apart for the gospel of God" (Romans 1:1). Just as in Paul's day, God still chooses particular individuals to do his work on a full-time basis.

It is a privilege and honor to be a called one. The first person who received the task to tell people about the risen Christ was Mary of Magdala (John 20:16–18). Throughout the ages, many have followed her example.

People cannot believe in a person of whom they have never heard. And hearing without preaching is impossible. "Consequently, faith comes from hearing the message, and the message is heard through the word of Christ" (Romans 10:17).

When Jesus prepared his twelve disciples to be sent out into his service, he first planned "that they might be with him" (Mark 3:14). That was a great characteristic by which people recognized them later on. When Peter and John were taken captive because of their preaching, the Jewish leaders were astonished at their boldness, and "they took note that these men had been with Jesus" (Acts 4:13). Their relationship with Jesus had inspired and enabled them in a difficult situation.

Jesus' commission to preach the gospel to the whole world and to make disciples in all nations still remains in force. Seen from God's point of view, the whole world is a mission field. Staying in your own country is not "second best" to going overseas. But because going to the mission field requires special preparation, I want to consider the call to be a missionary in detail with you.

Qualifications to Become a Missionary

I asked Dr. Frank Robbins, executive vice-president of the Wycliffe Bible Translators, "What, in your opinion, are the three most important conditions candidates need to fulfill before applying for mission work?" His carefully considered answer included preparation, perseverance, and partnership.

"First, someone has to be prepared to rely completely upon God. He will be tempted and get into crisis situations. Only if he has learned to cling to God, rather than being dependent upon man, will he be able to go through crises victoriously.

"Second, his motivation, dedication, and perseverance have to be so great that they can withstand time and difficulties. He must not run from seeming failure or fiasco. He can be this steadfast only if he knows he is personally called by God. It is just as big a calling to *stay* on the mission field as it is to *go* there.

"Third, it is necessary he be prepared to work as part of a team. He must be willing to accept leadership from others."

Struggles on the Mission Field

From twenty-five to fifty percent of missionaries do not return to the field after their first term. Studies indicate that there are two main defeats of the first-termer who doesn't return: He does not have a strong, personal relationship with God; and he is unable to get along with fellow missionaries.

Relationship with God

"The best preparation for the mission field? There is no doubt about that with me. It is maintaining a strong, daily relationship with God," says Tineke Bosch, Bible translator in Dutch Guyana. Since 1975 Tineke has been working on the translation of the Bible in Sarnami Hindustani. That is one of the fifteen languages spoken by the 140,000 people in Surinam, on the northeast coast of South America.

"Why did I go to the mission field? God called me," says Tineke. As a twenty-nine-year-old Dutch district nurse, Tineke had everything she could wish for in Holland: a fine job, a nice apartment, a good salary, many friends.

"But," she says, "I read about people who lived under a piece of cardboard; people who had no food for an entire day. In my work in child welfare as a nurse, we worked for hours to examine children who were already in good health, looking for something which could still be improved.

"Meanwhile, children around the world

were dying because they couldn't even receive the basic helps. Who would teach their mothers the first principles of hygiene and nutrition? Then I realized that these same symptoms were occurring on the spiritual level. In our home churches we were bickering about tiny, meaningless details, *while millions had never even heard the gospel.*"

That became the signal for Tineke to go and work as a nurse in a developing country. The transfer to missionary work was just the next step.

Living and working among people of a different culture is far from easy. "I need God's view on things," Tineke says. "That way my own view will be brought into balance, and I will see everything in proper proportions. The only recipe that keeps us on our feet in difficulties is daily Bible reading and prayer."

Something that helps missionaries like Tineke is prayer backing from her home country. All missionaries need small prayer cells who are informed about their needs and ministry, who will pray for them. They will then be *part* of the missionary work. It is wise to have been a member of such a group before leaving home. Then those in the group will consider the missionary one of their own.

Getting Along with Others
Gonnie Pothof, who works for the "Midnight Call" in Bolivia, says, "One of the most important things, especially for single women, is to be able

to live and work together with others. This is hard, especially when people have different ideas and customs, or if they have a totally different character than you have. It is particularly difficult at the outstations where one works for long periods of time with just a few other laborers. You all are relying upon your own resources, and this demands teamwork. And usually you don't select the partner you work with; he or she is assigned.

"Through the years I have had a variety of colaborers and have learned it is possible to work in unity in spite of great differences in personality. It is necessary, however, that we learn to ask forgiveness, and if differences of opinion arise— and they surely will—to look for errors within ourself first. If we cannot pray together and have no real love for each other, then it would be best to go home, for the ministry will become sterile."

Elze Stringer, who has worked for twenty-five years for the Alliance Mission in the interiors of Irian Jaya, says, "In dealing with other missionaries I receive great help from Philippians 2:3–4, which says we should consider others better than ourselves.

"When one thinks how deeply the Lord Jesus humbled himself for us, it becomes a bit easier to humble ourselves and to consider the other person higher, indeed. Then we can be willing to give up our desires for the greater cause, because he was willing to give up so much."

Culture Shock

This traumatic experience faced one missionary.

> Culture shock, what is it? I don't know how it is described in the dictionary, but for us it means crying and wanting to go home. It is to be angry with the people who have sent you out. It also means being rejected by one's surroundings.
>
> Fortunately this doesn't last long. For me it lasted about three months. When we departed the plane upon arrival in our new country, it seemed as if we had arrived in a soccer crowd. It was one pushing, shouting, sweating, irritated mass. I wondered if we, and our baggage, would even reach the airport exit unscathed.
>
> After that we drove to the ferry boat. Here again we were alarmed at being in what seemed to be an uncontrolled nation. There was no order, no politeness, no security. I felt very uncertain. Then in the evening when we drove through the town, everyone was sitting alongside the road with lighted candles. There were slum dwellings, cheap pubs, loud music, shouting, screaming—it was like a nightmare.
>
> Perhaps the house would give me security, I thought. But that was just as bad. Bars on the windows to discourage thieves. It was stifling hot inside . . . the heavy odor of sweat, the mosquito-netting, the stranger smells. The night noises: crickets, drums, shouts. Where am I? Why doesn't the shouting stop?
>
> The next morning: the garden has open sewage,

a rubbish hole and snakes. What about my children? The water has to be boiled. Fruit has to be cleaned thoroughly. The morning newspaper told about twelve persons hanged through a ritual slaughter.

You are tempted to give up, fearful of the hostile surroundings. You want to collapse, in spite of the fact that God has called you there.

After three months we had recovered from the worst shock. You learn to accept the situation. You realize why God has brought you here. He opened the doors. Thanks to His grace and the prayers of many people, we now begin to feel at home![1]

Loneliness

This is another struggle on the field. Elze Stringer says, "Sometimes I have to fight the feeling of loneliness. Often you are with only four Western missionaries at a station. If two of them are married and the third, your roommate, is quiet, then you will feel quite lonely. I'm not very talkative myself, so I need a 'talker' as a roommate.

"Married missionaries have a different kind of loneliness; it comes from sending their children off to school for the better part of the year."

Flexibility

Gonnie Pothof says, "I went to the mission field as a nurse. I loved the medical profession very much. However, God has changed the course of my ministry, and now I primarily do Bible instruction, training Bolivians to lead other people. God has given me great joy in this work, which I always thought I couldn't do. I have experienced the truth of Philippians 4:13—'I can do everything through him who gives me strength.'

"Whatever you can learn, in whatever area, learn it. It doesn't matter if it is about first aid, electricity, gardening, sewing, or laying bricks. You will find that it will all be helpful later on.

"It is important," she continues, "to be willing to do what has to be done when it needs to be done. You shouldn't leave home with too many fixed ideas. This flexibility will erase many inner conflicts."

Take an In-depth Personal Inventory

Many missionaries I have talked to stress the importance of good preparation. They say, "It sounds very adventuresome to go to the mission field and work for the Lord in an exotic land, but our experience has proven that it is all very difficult. You need to know very well what you are getting into."

Therefore, if you feel you are being called to the mission field, it is important to take the following inventory.

1. *How well do I know my Lord?*
   - Is he my Savior and my Lord?
   - Do I have a daily relationship with him?

- Do I dare to live with him alone? Can I keep going even if all other support leaves me?
- Have I learned to claim promises from the word?
- What place does his word have in my life? Do I have a well-balanced knowledge of the word?
- Do I practice what I know?
- Do I experience answers to my prayers?

2. *How well do I know myself?*
   - Are my motives pure?
   - Do I have a realistic insight about my gifts and limitations?
   - Considering my life in the light of the fruits of the Holy Spirit (Galations 5:22), do I possess love, so that I can associate with all sorts of people of different races and cultures?
   - Will I experience joy and peace if I have to give up things like the comfort and privacy I'm accustomed to?
   - Will I have patience if I should have to work for years before seeing fruit?
   - Am I flexible?
   - Am I open to learning new things?
   - How do I react to adverse situations?

3. *Am I prepared for my task?*
   - Am I well informed on the life and work of other missionaries?
   - Do I read books, biographies, and

prayer letters about them?
- How am I at learning a new language?
- Have I been in the practice of reaching my own countrymen with the gospel?
- Do I take opportunities to explain the gospel to people in their own language?

4. *How effectively do I work on my financial and prayer support?*
   - Do I have contact with a missionary group or society?
   - Am I a member of a prayer group?
   - Have I developed strong relationships and friendships with whom I can share my ministry later?
   - Do I have contact with a good Christian counselor?

With an honest self-examination of this sort, you will probably arrive at one conclusion: I am incapable! Here is where you must use Christ's strength, which is made perfect in your weakness. And you must remember that God has called you to this work. He qualifies the people he wants to be on the field. Also, you must allow yourself room for growth. Jesus' disciples were simple men, but they helped transform the world! They were men who became his messengers because they had been his companions first.

NOTES
1. "The Harvest" ("De Oogst") *Trouw/Kwartet*, July 2, 1979, page 2.

QUESTIONS FOR STUDY AND APPLICATION

1. Write a summary about proclaiming the gospel based on Mark 16:15, Matthew 28:19–20, and Acts 1:8. How does 1 Corinthians 15:1–5 describe the contents of the gospel?

2. Study the following verses to learn the different ways a person can contribute to the Great Commission: Isaiah 6:8, Matthew 9:37–38, 2 Corinthians 9:1–5, and Philippians 4:15–18.

3. Read Romans 12:3–8 and 1 Corinthians 12:4–11 and prayerfully list the gift(s) you feel God has given you.

4. Think about Mark 10:28–30 and 2 Corinthians 9:6–8, then paraphrase the verses. According to Mark 3:14–15 and Acts 4:13, what should characterize the life of a messenger of Christ?

5. List what the women in Romans 16:1–16 did to further the gospel. Read Acts 18:1–4 and 18–28 to see what else is stated about Priscilla.

6. What have you learned that will enable you to help make known the gospel? How and when will you make a start using what you have learned?

Extra study: In John 17 Jesus prayed for the people who were his companions and messengers. Read this chapter and answer the following questions. What did Jesus say about them? What did he pray for them? In what ways did he expect them to be his messengers?

12

BEFORE YOU SAY "I DO"

Apart from saying "Yes, Lord" when she surrenders herself completely to Christ, there are no more important words for a young woman than the words *I do*, which she speaks to her husband on their wedding day.

On that day she changes her name (usually), civil status, and often her profession. She also gives up certain freedoms. As she enters this new relationship in life, she knows neither its duration nor its circumstances.

If, as is often the case, she marries a man she knows only superficially, she is indeed embarking on a dangerous venture. Solomon says in Proverbs 19:2, "It is not good to have zeal without knowledge, nor to be hasty and miss the way." There are few areas of life in which this verse is more applicable than in marriage.

In the business world, no pains are spared to minimize risk. Businessmen gather all sorts of information before making decisions. Long questionnaires need to be completed and medical and psychological reports prepared before hiring a new employee. References are requested and interviews are conducted. There may even be a handwriting analysis in some cases. And all that is at stake is a job, a situation one can change any day.

Our present society reveals a low esteem of marriage; in America the divorce rate is now about fifty percent. Tens of thousands of others don't even get married. They just live together!

Christians, if anyone, can offer new hope to the world by maintaining stable marriages and solid families. The first step is to establish marriage on the principles God has laid down in his word.

Questions to Answer Before You Marry

There is certain disaster if a man and woman don't approach marriage seriously. Nothing weakens your discernment as much as being in love. Love (or what one often thinks is love) has a tendency to cover up the faults of the beloved. Therefore, sound guidelines must be followed.

What must be considered in order to make the proper decision?

Is He a Christian?
The Bible says a Christian woman "is free to marry anyone she wishes, but he must belong to the Lord" (1 Corinthians 7:39). A husband and wife must build on the same foundation—Jesus Christ. They must be one in this most essential and deepest matter of life. The word of God must have the same value for both partners; they must navigate with the same compass.

Paul gives an unequivocal warning about marrying an unbeliever.

> Do not be unequally yoked up with unbelievers—
> do not make mismated alliances with them,
> or come under a different yoke with them [in-
> consistent with your faith]. For what partnership
> have right living and right standing with God
> with iniquity and lawlessness? Or how can light
> fellowship with darkness? (2 Corinthians 6:14,
> *The Amplified New Testament*).

There is probably no greater curse than a bad marriage. The warnings are clear in the Bible, but they must be put into practice. A woman may think that she will surely win the unbelieving man she loves to Christ, once they are married. But God cannot bless an alliance that he has expressly forbidden. Marriage is not the vehicle for evangelism and conversion.

A woman who marries an unbelieving man

stands little chance that he will come to Christ. And there is the risk that if they have children, they will follow in the father's non-Christian footsteps. Jesus said, "By their fruit you will recognize them" (Matthew 7:16). A good tree produces good fruit; a bad tree produces bad fruit.

What an immense responsibility to bring people into being, then risk having them lost for eternity.

Do You Share the Same Spiritual Interests?

Unity in the faith is necessary, but not sufficient. Happiness in marriage is largely dependent on the spiritual maturity of the couple. It is difficult to live together if one spouse puts a greater value on the word and prayer than the other one does. One wife said to me, "We do pray and read the Bible together, but I always have to take the initiative. I feel that my husband would not really like to do it at all."

Then there is the marriage in which the man feels called to the service of God. As a woman, you have to be careful not to be jealous of the time your husband spends on spiritual matters.

Is There Harmony of Character?

Too great a difference in character and temperament can produce tension, while equal temperaments can clash as well.

Love must be based on mutual respect and understanding. There needs to be room for fellowship and open discussion. One woman said,

"One of the mates must be able to provide what the other is missing."

Another woman said, "I want someone on the same level. He must be able to understand me. There *must* be an exchange of thoughts." Yet, as another friend suggested, "There must also be room for each to develop a life of his own."

An older woman shared, "Our marriage went wrong because my husband was jealous of me and my accomplishments."

Do You Have Mutual Interests?

Be sure there isn't too great a difference in basic education. Can you challenge one another on the intellectual level? Do you share any common sports or hobbies?

The more mutual exchange there is, the stronger the unity of the marriage relationship will be. This will also help keep the marriage new and fresh.

How Do Your Backgrounds Compare?

It is important not only to get to know one another, but to get acquainted with each other's background, as well. Differences in language, nationality, social background, education, and church affiliation are not insurmountable, but they do put extra pressure on the marriage and should be carefully considered. Initially it may appear that the hindrances can be overcome, but later they develop into a wedge between the couple.

Another good question to ask is how the

young man's father behaves towards his wife and children. There is a good chance that the son will behave in a similar way.

An issue that causes a great deal of trouble in many marriages is finances. Get to know one another's spending habits. If there are wide differences, can they be bridged? Discuss this openly during courtship.

A Cinderella who marries a prince sounds nice as a fairy tale, but in practice it could be a disaster. One marriage consultant says, "Refuse to think of marrying someone who differs too greatly with you in background. Love doesn't solve all problems. It never has and it never will. Moreover, love is only one of the many aspects of a happy marriage."

What Do Counselors Think?

The Bible is very positive about gathering information: "The way of a fool seems right to him, but a wise man listens to advice" (Proverbs 12:15). "Plans fail for lack of counsel, but with many advisers they succeed" (Proverbs 15:22).

Gathering information doesn't mean that others can make decisions for us. We must decide for ourselves, for we are held responsible before God. But it is important that as much light as possible is shed on such an important matter as marriage. Why not take advantage of the counsel of wise men and women?

Use the principles set forth in chapter three about finding God's will. Counsel is one of those steps.

Above all else, don't forget to consult your parents. "Honor your father and mother" is a commandment with a promise; "that it may go well with you" (Ephesians 6:2–3).

As late as the nineteenth century, marriage in Western nations was generally a decision between the two families. For a majority of the people in the world, it still is. It may sound strange to those of us in the West, but studies have shown that marriages in which the parents were not consulted were less successful than those in which they were consulted!

God honors obedience to his word, which says, "Listen to your father, who gave you life, and do not despise your mother when she is old" (Proverbs 23:22). Heeding the advice of parents is not restricted to childhood.

Your Marriage Partner Should Also Be Your Friend

When I said "Yes, I do" to Aart Karssen, I thought, "It is wonderful that he will become my husband, for I love him deeply. But it is too bad that I will now lose a good friend." But, fortunately, this was not the case.

During our courtship a strong friendship developed between us. The fact that many miles separated us did not have a bearing on our friendship. We continued to get to know each other's thoughts, opinions, and interests.

It was only later that I understood that friendship is the best start for a marriage, and that I had not lost a friend in my husband. Falling in love is important, of course, but friendship is even more lasting, more durable. Love is fed and enriched by it.

It is a pity that the courtship time is becoming increasingly shorter these days. This simply does not allow for two people to get to know one another very well. To get married too quickly deprives the couple of something beautiful. This can cause damage to a marriage that can't be repaired. It is difficult to make up for lost time.

Many newlyweds would experience fewer problems by taking time for more preparation. Mutual experiences, socializing, getting acquainted with each other's relatives, and simply talking help develop a bond that the marriage will need later.

QUESTIONS FOR STUDY AND APPLICATION

1. What do the following verses teach as background for marriage? Genesis 2:18–24, Malachi 2:15–16, Matthew 19:5–6, Romans 7:2–3, Hebrews 13:4

2. Read 1 Corinthians 7:39 and 2 Corinthians 6:14.
   a. What is the first condition to be fulfilled in a Christian marriage?
   b. What warning does God give in Deuteronomy 7:3–4, 1 Kings 11:1–3, and Ezra 9:1–2 against marrying an unbeliever?

3. By which fruits do we know if someone is a Christian? Matthew 7:21, Romans 1:13 and 6:22, Galatians 5:22, and Hebrews 12:11 and 13:15

4. What does the Bible teach about listening to counselors? Look up Proverbs 11:14, 12:15, 13:10, 15:22, and 23:22.

5. What advice do the following verses give? Psalm 119:105, Romans 12:2, Ephesians 5:17, James 1:5

6. What have you learned about marriage that you can apply to your circumstances?

13

BASICS FOR A MARRIAGE TO WORK

"Without Christ, marriage is a gamble," said my English friend, Barbara. It was a bright morning in June. We were sitting in her garden, a garden like those only the English country houses have; a large, smooth lawn with colorful borders of flowers and rustling trees. Restful!

Though her statement applies to all aspects of human life, it does especially apply to marriage. "You suffer damage," she continued, "if you are content with less than doing God's perfect will."

To Barbara, God's perfect will means a willingness to adapt herself to her husband in *obedience*. "This doesn't mean that I should be a doormat. I enjoy the fact that Victor is over me. It gives me rest and security. I can look up to him," she said.

I smiled to myself. It was impossible to see this lovely, well-dressed woman as a doormat. She has traveled the world as the wife of an executive in an international company. As a Christian woman, she is widely appreciated for her spiritual ministry.

Submission to the Husband

Why would a woman who can manage herself very well choose to be submissive to her husband? Because the Bible commands this, and because a woman is happier in the long run if she obeys what God commands of her. Disobedience always brings frustration, for it breaks her relationship with God.

Paul wrote in Ephesians 5:21–24,

> Submit to one another out of reverence for Christ.
> Wives, submit to your husbands as to the Lord.
> For the husband is the head of the wife as Christ
> is the head of the church, his body, of which
> he is the Savior. Now as the church submits to
> Christ, so also wives should submit to their hus-
> bands in everything.

The Bible leaves no room for exceptions. Then, as Ephesians 5:25–33 explains, the husband, too, has a responsibility to love his wife as he loves himself; to cherish her as his own body.

The Bible explicitly says a woman is to be submissive to her *own* husband only, not to every man. Therefore, in church and in society, the married woman has the authority which is given to her position. Think of a female police officer or of the biblical examples of Deborah and Huldah. Only within the marriage relationship is the woman asked to submit to the man.

No one can compel a woman to marry a particular man. She has the opportunity to choose her own husband. Author Elizabeth Rice Handford asks, "Did you ever realize how lucky you are, that you can choose the man you marry and obey? You didn't get the opportunity to choose your parents and yet had to obey them. You couldn't choose the teachers whom you had to obey. You have, actually, little choice with regard to the public authorities whom you obey. But only the most comprehensive and direct authority in your life—that authority you may choose."[1]

The question a woman must ask herself before she marries is whether or not she is willing to obey this man as her husband. She enjoys two privileges: First, she is free to choose her husband; second, she is free to obey him.

Nowhere in the Bible is the man to command that his wife submit to him. His sacrificing love and care for her should be so encouraging that she freely gives her obedience to him. He must deserve his leadership.

"I will have difficulty accepting a man as my leader, because I am inclined to push myself forward," said a girl in a small group Bible study.

She isn't the only girl with that attitude! It is one of the strangest contradictions in a woman, that on the one hand she wants a man she can look up to, yet she attempts to undermine his authority once she has found him!

Each of us has a strong streak of rebellion against authority. By nature we are all autocrats. We want to rule ourselves, with no one else interfering.

But if a woman thinks it is difficult to submit to the authority of her husband, just look at what God asks of the husband. His assignment is the most difficult of the two. The husband is expected *to love his wife as Christ loved his church*, which means he should even be willing to die for her.

God gave man to be the leader of the wife, but this does not indicate superiority. According to God's order of creation, woman is equal to man. She makes him complete. She helps him where he cannot help himself.

The man is not a master over the woman. He is her head. Because husband and wife become one flesh in marriage, there can only be one head—the man. And he is thus responsible to God. We saw this with Adam and Eve after she sinned. God didn't call her to account, but Adam (Genesis 3).

Marriage is a teamwork situation; decisions should be made after joint input and discussion. The greater the input of both parties, the more successful the decision will be.

When there is a difference of opinion, the

man makes the final decision, provided, of course, that his decision is not contrary to God's word.

"I obey, even if Victor is wrong," says Barbara. "God is above everything, isn't he? When I give in, Victor sometimes says later, 'You were right!' This is a matter of faith. If God wants you to do a certain thing, he will work it out in your husband. But my disobedience can stand in God's way. It can prevent his purpose being achieved."

This is an answer to the question women often ask themselves: "What do I do if my husband makes a wrong decision?" Men, being human, will naturally make mistakes. "But I have also noticed that God often changes my thoughts on certain decisions," a husband once told me.

God gives the man and woman the key to open their way to happiness—Jesus Christ. Living in the reverence of Christ means that both partners freely decide, out of love, to do his will and to be guided by the example of Christ who freely gave up his rights. He only wanted to do the will of God (Philippians 2:5–8).

Only out of love for Christ can a woman learn to obey her husband, and in so doing she obeys her Lord. And only out of love for Christ can a man love his wife as himself, and in that way express his love to Jesus Christ. When a man shows this kind of love, shouldn't the wife be willing to adapt herself to him?

Again, the crux of the matter is in choosing the right man—a man who has the possibilities within him to be able to properly lead. Remember, the man is also a sinner, and he will need to grow into mature leadership in the marriage. As the man grows spiritually, he will become aware that he needs his wife to help him become the man God wants him to be.

Seven Basic Needs in a Marriage

Some years ago The Navigators in The Netherlands held a one-day conference for young couples. The speaker was Jim White, from America. He gave seven basic needs that husbands and wives both have. Most of the problems in marriage develop, according to Jim, because these needs are neglected. In nature, weeds will come up of themselves and run wild if not controlled. A marriage also needs continuous care if it is to bear good fruit.

Here are Jim's conclusions.

Acceptance
Let the other partner know that you are happy with him or her. Allow the other person to be himself. It means emphasizing his strong points rather than dwelling on his weak points. It implies making no extreme demands nor comparison with other couples!

Accepting the partner means doing so with love and patience, as Christ accepted us (Romans 15:7).

The first step enabling one to do this is faith. You must have the faith that you are first accepted by God. If you aren't sure about this, you will have a difficult time accepting your partner.

Appreciation

Appreciation needs to be *expressed*. It can become easy to take the other for granted, to no longer say "thank you."

Why is appreciation so important? Because it is a reflection of our response to the character of God. God likes to be thanked (1 Thessalonians 5:18). In the Old and New Testaments, people who weren't grateful were severely punished (Deuteronomy 28:47–48 and Romans 1:21).

Marriage dries up a little bit if there is no appreciation expressed, even for the little things. In fact, it is the "little" things that are so important.

Develop an attitude of gratitude for your entire life. Use part of your daily quiet time to thank God. And thank your mate at least once a day for something he has done.

Encouragement

Everyone needs encouragement from time to time. He desires to know that he is valuable, that he is doing a good job. This invigorates his feeling of self-esteem, and at the same time enlarges his capacity. Too often we dwell on the weak qualities rather than emphasizing strengths. Most people become what you expect them to be.

Jim gives four practical suggestions to encourage our partner: Be a good listener; give sincere compliments; don't be critical; and never say no unless it is absolutely necessary.

Consideration

It is important to give attention to one another, to be courteous and kind. Jesus is our example. He washed the feet of his disciples even though it was not customary that this was done by a fellow guest. Every Jewish home had a small room where one could wash his own feet. Those who were rich had a servant do it. When Jesus washed the disciples' feet, it was an act of practical kindness. He was an example of one willing to serve.

We do a lot when we are courting to win the love of someone. But within marriage we seem to forget to give the flowers, the candy, the card—the attention—that we gave when we sought each other's love.

The scriptural standard for dealing with others is Matthew 7:12—"In everything, do to others what you would have them to do to you." A practical suggestion in this respect is to do one thing each day for your mate that goes beyond normal obligations.

Communication

By communication I mean not only the verbal type, but also the non-verbal process between two people by which they know they are being listened to, and that they are being seriously and understood.

Many adults communicate in the same way their parents did. God does not intend that we copy the parental home unless the communication there was based on love and done with skill.

Some of the enemies of communication are egoism, lack of forgiveness, and the fear of not being accepted. But, interestingly enough, marriage counselors say that fifty percent of all problems in communication result from silence from the husband. After a day of talking with other people in his business, he wants to relax. His wife, to the contrary, may have spent the day with small children (or alone) and wants to talk when the husband comes home.

Both needs are legitimate. Therefore, it is necessary that the couple plan to help each other.

Physical Affection
The need for physical affection was God's idea. He gave this desire to man and woman. Paul wrote that husbands and wives should not rule over their own bodies, but give love to their spouse (1 Corinthians 7:3–5).

The expression of physical love ranges from a gentle touch to becoming completely one. God gave sex in order for man and woman to intensely enjoy their love for one another. Husbands and wives must pray about this and then in an act of devotional surrender offer their bodies to God and to one another.

Leadership
A woman has a unique need and desire for guidance from her husband. This does not mean he is to be a dictator who makes arbitrary decisions or who always thinks he is right.

A good leader is someone who makes justified decisions. He is an example and sets the tone in the relationship with God. He is the high priest in his own house. He doesn't make all the decisions himself, but he does take the final responsibility. He must also be able to delegate some responsibility.

The man cannot demand this leadership; it must be given to him by the woman. She must allow him to be her leader. If she does so, she helps her husband develop himself. There is little that encourages him more than the knowledge that his wife is one with him. If a woman adapts herself in faith to her husband, it will lead to a harmonious marriage.

God not only established marriage but also gave directives to make it successful. People who take God's commandments seriously in the daily practice of their marriage are choosing a good marriage—and happiness!

NOTES

1. Elizabeth Rice Handford, *Me? Obey Him?* (Sword of the Lord Publishers, 1979). Dutch translation by Uit het Woord der Waarheid, Winschoten (the Netherlands, 1975), page 64.

QUESTIONS FOR STUDY AND APPLICATION
In order to answer questions one, two, and three, read Ephesians 5:21–33 through several times.

1. What is the image of the marriage relationship of the husband and wife?
   a. What is expected of both?
   b. How should the woman express her responsibilities?
   c. How should the man express his?

2. In what way does a woman have to be submissive to her husband?

3. Write down all the things that God expects of a man in regard to his wife.

4. According to Titus 2:5, what is the purpose of submissiveness?
   a. Read 1 Peter 3:1 to learn what can happen if a woman is submissive to her unbelieving husband.
   b. What can you do to become more humble? (Read 1 Peter 5:5–7.)

5. What does 1 Corinthians 11:3 call the man in regard to the woman? What do you think this means?
   What do we learn from the example of Christ that can be applied in marriage? Read Matthew 26:39, John 4:34, Philippians 2:1–9, and Hebrews 5:8.

6. What have you learned in this chapter about the marriage relationship that can help you in the situation you are in?

14

THE GIFT OF REMAINING SINGLE

"We advised Susanne to seriously consider remaining single," her father said.

Susanne is twenty years old. She hasn't
written off her chances of getting married; in fact,
she has already had one proposal of marriage.

"Susanne is very capable at evangelism," her
father continued. "The Lord has exceptionally
blessed her in it. On the basis of what Paul writes
to the Corinthians, we know that for some people marriage isn't the first, but the second choice.
Some are simply happiest remaining single. That
is their gift, just as other people have the gift of
marriage. Before someone decides that remaining single is absolutely not for them, I think it

would be best to study the truths of 1 Corinthians 7."

Susanne's father isn't an opponent of marriage. On the contrary, he and his wife have one of the most harmonious marriages I have observed. Nor does he underestimate the happiness and blessings of having a family, for he is a father who fully enjoys his children. However, he and his wife know that marriage and all it provides does not give the greatest happiness on earth. The greatest happiness comes from doing God's will.

Why Being Single Can Be a Blessing

Paul wrote about singleness in 1 Corinthians 7: "I wish that all men were as I am. But each man has his own gift from God; one has this gift, another has that." These are remarkable words for a single person. We usually hear the opposite. It is so important that we pay full attention to Paul's unexpected statement. How can he speak so positively about being single? Why is he not bitter? What is his secret?

The secret is in the word *gift*. God gives some the gift of being able to remain single.

We know that Paul was single when he wrote this. He saw his own position as a privilege; this was not a fanatical statement *against* marriage. He respected the institution and considered it as established by God. But the privilege he had was that of complete freedom to devote *all his days* as an apostle to the service of God. There were no human ties to prevent him from doing this.

The World Clamors for Marriage

Paul was certainly out of step with what we hear around us. The world tries to convince us in a myriad of ways that an intimate relationship with the opposite sex is synonymous with happiness. We are bombarded daily with this on the radio and television, and in films, literature, and popular songs. Singles are given names with inferior connotations: spinster, old maid. No wonder so many young people, Christians included, think that life is bypassing them if they remain single for too long.

Perhaps even Christian couples unconsciously harbor the idea that marriage is the rule and that singleness is an exception or deficiency. This certainly causes single people to feel they are outside the norm of society. They often feel more tolerated than wanted.

Whereas the Roman Catholic church idealizes singleness by placing celibacy above marriage, in Protestant churches there is too little attention and appreciation for the single person. In his book *Marriage Weighed*, J. van Bruggen asks, "Why doesn't the church teach that the single Christian man or woman is not a subject of compassion, but a full-fledged and privileged fellow traveler on the way in which we are all called to please our God?"[1]

The Gift of Life

These wrong attitudes toward singleness can be changed by thinking scripturally. We then will see being married or single from the perspective of our whole reason for existence—to glorify God.

God gives us the gift of life. This life can be lived in either the married or single state. Both are equal gifts of God. You do not earn a gift; you receive it. Nor is a gift something to pride oneself on. Neither should we look down on someone else just because he has a different gift. All gifts are for the benefit of the body and all are handed out freely by the Giver (1 Corinthians 12).

The gift of marriage does seem to be the rule and the gift of remaining single the exception. *Yet they are equal and complete each other.* That is how God has set up his kingdom! Neither can be left out of the larger picture. Marriage is essential for the propagation of the earth. On the other hand, single women can accomplish those tasks for which married women have no time or are incapable.

Think of how different the mission field would be if there had not been a multitude of single female missionaries, who through the years have performed tasks for which there were no others available. The special influence of the single woman is not restricted to the mission field, but can be found in every strata of society.

Who Are the Ones Who Can Remain Single?

Who are the people who perhaps should seriously consider remaining single? What are the advantages, and what aims can be achieved? Paul gives answers in 1 Corinthians 7.

For people to whom sexual desire is not a continuous tension and temptation, Paul feels it is good not to marry. It is not only good, it is even better.

As Paul gives four reasons to remain single, he places these reasons in the context of the imminent return of Christ; the time to serve God is short because the present world order is passing away (verses 25, 29–31).

To avoid the troubles of life. Paul realized that "those who marry will face many troubles in this life" (7:28), and he wanted to spare them that.

To be free from concern and anxiety. He also wrote, "I would like you to be free from concern" (7:32). The *Amplified New Testament* translation is, "My desire is to have you free from all anxiety and distressing care." He explained that "a married man is concerned about the affairs of this world—how he can please his wife—and his interests are divided" (7:33,34).

The married Christian woman lives with the tension between her responsibilities to her family and her responsibilities to God. For such a woman, it is much more difficult to give God first place than it is for the single woman. Life is more complicated. She is being pulled in two directions.

As a Christian, it is certainly her duty to accomplish her tasks as a wife, for the glory of God. One study revealed that married women spend a great amount of time worrying about the health of their husbands. Jesus warned that it is exactly this type of worry about earthly things that chokes the word in the human heart and makes it unfruitful (Mark 4:19).

To devote oneself to the Lord. Paul continued, "An unmarried woman or virgin is concerned about the Lord's affairs: Her aim is to be devoted to the Lord in both body and spirit" (7:34).

This is not an automatic thing; it is a matter of choice. A single woman *can* spend her time in many other ways. But her circumstances make it possible to be more available to God.

Some tasks are open *only* to the single woman. A story is told of two female missionaries of the Wycliffe Bible Translators in South America. An Indian chief in Peru told a missionary official, "If you had sent men, we would have killed them on sight. Or if a couple, I'd have killed the man and taken the woman for myself. But what could a great chief do with two harmless girls who insisted on calling him 'brother?' (Tribal law of the Shapra Indians was that men must always defend their sisters.)"[2]

To be happier. In referring to a widow, Paul said, "In my judgment, she is happier if she stays as she is" (7:40). Women who have *accepted* singleness, whatever the reason, often show a striking poise, peace, and usefulness.

But what about those women who remain single out of necessity, not because they have to do so? For them the answer lies in verse thirty-five: "I am saying this for your own good, not to restrict you, but that you may live in a right way in *undivided devotion* to the Lord." To fulfill this aim makes the single person *happy.*

But if a woman thinks that the gift of being single is not meant for her, she may find peace in these words of Jesus: "Your Father in heaven [will] give good gifts to those who ask him" (Matthew 7:11). "But seek first his kingdom and his righteousness, and all these things will be given to you as well" (Matthew 6:33). We must take the Bible seriously in this respect. God says we have not because we ask not (James 4:2). A single woman can pray for a husband with great boldness.

God is a God of surprises. He wants to give us his best, that which makes us happiest. But we must turn ourselves over to him completely, desiring first his honor and glory. This is the condition for every answer to prayer. When we do this, we will see that whatever gift he gives us will suit us best. His gift will be, at the same time, a gift and an assignment!

NOTES
1. J. van Bruggen, *Marriage Weighed (Het Huwelijk Gewogen)* (Amsterdam: Ton Bolland, 1979), page 39.
2. Dorothy R. Pape, *In Search of God's Ideal Woman* (Inter-Varsity Press, 1976), page 262.

QUESTIONS FOR STUDY AND APPLICATION

1. Read 1 Corinthians 12:4–27.
   a. Who gives the gifts?
   b. Why are they given?
   c. What warnings are given with them?

2. What does Paul mean in 1 Corinthians 7:7 when he mentions the word *gift*?

3. Describe the gift of remaining single.

4. Read 1 Corinthians 7:29–35. For what reasons does Paul think it is better for people with the gift of being single not to marry? What are some of your own thoughts?

5. What disadvantages does this gift have?

6. Read Philippians 4:6–7 and Ephesians 3:20. What should a single woman do when she realizes she doesn't have the gift of sexual abstinence?

7. List all the advantages of being single, according to 1 Corinthians 7.

Extra study: Summarize what you have learned from this study as if you were telling it to someone else. Perhaps there is someone you can serve by sharing this information.

15

WHEN WIDOWHOOD OCCURS

"I thought it wouldn't happen to me," said my friend Jenny, whom I had not seen in quite some time. That was her answer to my simple question, "How are you?" She had just lost her husband, a well-known evangelist, who had been a blessing to countless people.

What happened to her that she couldn't believe was not the loss of her husband, but being deserted by former friends. People, especially couples, who used to visit her regularly, no longer came.

This situation is a frequent complaint of widows. Sometimes this is the widow's fault, but more often it is the others' fault. As I listened to Jenny, I realized that I had more pity for the people who had deserted her than I did for Jenny. This was because she had obviously found her way again in spite of her sorrow. As a human being, she undoubtedly had more to offer now than before. She would be able to help others with what she had learned—if only they would give her a chance.

I don't know why people desert widows. Maybe it is because they simply don't know how to cope with the sorrow of others. Are they fleeing their own fear by ignoring someone who is left alone?

"I was glad she didn't notice me in the supermarket," a woman said about a friend who had just become a widow, "for I wouldn't know what to say to her." What this woman didn't realize—perhaps couldn't know because of her lack of experience—is that someone who has just suffered a great loss doesn't necessarily need words. A look or a squeeze of the hand are often quite sufficient.

Many widows are unnecessarily wounded by the little misunderstandings of others. But to keep in touch with couples can be the balm for her wounded heart. She needs the male input from other couples, for she suddenly misses her husband's influence in her own life.

The American author Katie F. Wiebe writes, "Like most widows, I found the fact that I was now an incomplete social unit one of the first difficult adjustments. . . . When I was invited to the homes of women my own age, it was usually when their husbands were away for business trips or other reasons.

"Although most married couples won't admit it openly," she says, "being married does make them feel superior to single persons."[1]

The reaction of the widow to this type of treatment often is that she will withdraw. If that happens, she will become completely secluded in her sorrow. When she cannot think or talk about anything else, it is a dangerous state.

Catherine Marshall, widow of the well-known minister, Peter Marshall, wrote,

> When a deep injury to the spirit has been sustained, the tendency of the sorrowing is to shut the heart and bar the door lest hurt be heaped upon hurt. Yet isolation is not the way toward mental health. Of course, the newly bereaved person needs periods of stabilizing solitude both for physical rest and to gain perspective. But in between times, he needs to accept as fully as he can the love that flows from friends and family. . . .
>
> Yet it is God alone who can finally heal the brokenhearted. Grief is a real wound, a mutilation, a gaping hole in the human spirit. After all, the ties that bind parents to children, brothers to sisters, and husbands to wives are the deepest of bonds, as real as love is real. Some beloved person has been wrested, torn bodily from one's life. The hurt is none the less real because the family physician cannot probe it; Christ alone is physician to the spirit.[2]

Indeed, Jesus Christ, who thoroughly knows

the human heart because he created it, is the only one who gauges its deepest need. David wrote, "Trust in him at all times, O people; pour out your hearts to him" (Psalm 62:8). "The Lord heals the brokenhearted and binds up their wounds" (Psalm 147:3).

The Reality of Sorrow

What is interesting about these two widowed authors is that they frankly admitted the extent of their sorrow. Often people think it is "Christian" to cover up any sorrows. They think that Christians should not cry. This is a gross misconception. Christians shouldn't minimize their sorrow, for that can even retard the process of healing. Call sorrow what it is, without feeling any guilt about it.

How does one carry on without collapsing? By claiming the promises of God. The Bible has a message for people who are bereaved. It says that sorrow and trouble belong to this life.

Peter was very clear about this aspect of the Christian life. He wrote, "Dear friends, do not be surprised at the painful trial you are suffering, as though something strange were happening to you" (1 Peter 4:12).

Isaiah, eight hundred years before Peter, gave the same message: "When you pass through the waters, I will be with you; and when you pass through the rivers, they will not sweep over you. When you walk through the fire, you will not be burned; the flames will not set you ablaze. For I am the Lord, your God, the Holy One of Israel, your Saviour" (Isaiah 43:2–3). The biblical message is not that there won't be any problems, but that we will be helped in the midst of our problems.

The Potential of Sorrow

Sorrow is never an end in itself. God allows it in your life with the intention that it open a new stage of living. He closes one door to open another. Joseph went from the pit via Potiphar's house and jail to the position of governor of Egypt (Genesis 37 and 39–45). Even Jesus' exaltation was preceded by humiliation (Philippians 2:6–11).

There is potential within sorrow. Romans 8:28 teaches, "And we know that in all things God works for the good of those who love him, who have been called according to his purpose." "All things" includes being a widow.

But the potential good won't happen automatically. Our voluntary participation is essential. This implies something different for each person.

What a challenge! There is probably no more moving example of positive growth from sorrow than that of Job and his wife. Death struck tenfold with them; their seven sons and three daughters all perished at the same time.

The parents reacted differently. Job's wife

closed the door of her life. She saw no more reasons to live.

But Job refused to give up. He gained a deeper perspective from the suffering. In the beginning, as with most of us, Job did not understand the meaning of it all. It was a mystery. But he did not doubt God! The consequences? At the end of his life, Job was a much richer person than before. The price was high and the way he had to go seemed impossible.

Through Job we can see that even though the worst occurs, there still is a God. And he is a God who helps and who cares, who carries you through. He is a God who in his infinite goodness can give the most brokenhearted person a new beginning.

Practical Preparation

Mary's husband was upstairs putting the children to bed. We could hear their excited voices of delight as they were tickled, loved, and tucked in.

Mary and I were doing the dishes and discussing widowhood.

"Strange," said my hostess, who was thirty-two years old, "I always think that it won't happen to me." She and her husband were young. The day of widowhood that she might have to face did indeed seem far away to her.

Then I talked with a sixty-year-old widow. She said the same thing as Mary. "John and I did everything together. Subconsciously I thought we would also pass away at the same time. It was a foolish thought, actually, for he had already had one light heart attack. I should have been warned by that."

Every woman, young or old, seems to push the thought of widowhood out of her mind. No one can blame her for that! Yet a wife who has not given some thought to widowhood is less prepared for marriage than one who doesn't know how to change a baby's diaper.

Not to think about widowhood is to be short-sighted. Illness and death are a part of our earthly existence. And because the average woman lives longer than a man and usually marries a man older than herself, it is probably the woman who is left behind.

Furthermore, because the life expectancy of a woman is longer, she will be a widow for a longer period of time than ever before. In 1960, for example, the average American woman became widowed at sixty-four. This means she still had about fifteen years of her life to live—alone. In 1970, only ten years later, her years of widowhood had risen to eighteen.

Every day in The Netherlands 180 women are left alone through widowhood or divorce. On January 1, 1978 there were 577,696 widows and 152,422 divorced women. This means that more than five percent of the Dutch population of 14,000,000 consisted of former married women now alone.

There is no family in the world unaffected

by death. This doesn't mean a married woman should live in daily fear of losing her husband, for then she wouldn't have a single day of happy marriage. Also, the Bible expressly warns us against worry of any kind and advises us to live one day at a time (Matthew 6:25–34). It also encourages us to live by faith, not by fear (Hebrews 10:38). But these warnings are not an excuse to be unthinking or careless about the future. Solomon said, "No one has power over the day of his death" (Ecclesiastes 8:8). Trying to contain death is as foolish as trying to catch the wind in your hand.

But it is important to make some preparations so that when widowhood occurs, the sadness won't be further complicated by unnecessary frustrations which could have been foreseen. This isn't an exhaustive list, but it does provide some basic suggestions for what you can do now.

Understand your finances. The wife should cosign the checks. This will enable her to pay the expenses that accompany death and often need to be paid immediately. All financial arrangements, if possible, should be in both the husband's and wife's names. A husband should explain to his wife all of his business and legal affairs.

Write a will. If a man has a business of his own and passes away before making a will, this will present terrible financial and legal problems. Make a will now, even though the thought of death is far away.

Develop independent capabilities. A woman

who has had some independence before her marriage and has looked after her own affairs will be stronger and more capable in life if she becomes a widow. The better she is prepared, the better balanced she will be in her reaction to death.

Hezekiah, king of Judah, was told, "Put your house in order, because you will die" (2 Kings 20:1). This is a warning each of us must heed. Don't worry about it, but take it as one of the normal preparations of life, as one of the necessities of existence.

NOTES

1. Katie F. Wiebe, *Alone—A Widow's Search for Joy* (Tyndale House Publishers, 1976), pages 46–47.
2. Catherine Marshall, *To Live Again* (McGraw Hill, 1957), pages 46–47.

QUESTIONS FOR STUDY AND APPLICATION

1. For what two things does each person have to prepare himself? Read 2 Corinthians 5:10 and Hebrews 9:27.

2. What encouragement do you receive from the following verses if you are suffering difficulties or sorrow? 1 Corinthians 10:13, 2 Corinthians 4:17–18, Revelation 21:3–5

3. Study the prayer of Moses in Psalm 90. What parts of this prayer seem applicable to widowhood in some way? Memorize verse twelve.

4. Study Matthew 6:25–34, Hebrews 10:38, and Philippians 4:6–7. What can you learn and apply about worrying and being anxious?

5. Talk to widows you know who have capably dealt with the loss of their husband. List the key points to remember should you ever become a widow.

6. With your husband go step by step through all business, legal, and other affairs that you would be left with if he should die.

7. Read some books on widowhood and do those things suggested for dealing with it.

Extra study: Study the widows of the Bible to see how they handled their sorrow.

16

ACCEPTING WIDOWHOOD

It was a bright summer day over thirty years ago. The grounds of the Christian conference center swarmed with laughing boys and girls at their annual youth camp.

This particular afternoon was sports time, although sports were just one aspect of the camp. The particular aim was to talk to the young people about their personal relationship to Jesus Christ. We wanted to help them make important choices in life, decisions which, if made in these early years, would have far-reaching significance.

I entered the large conference building and noticed a young woman who had recently become a widow. I didn't know her but had heard about her sorrow. Her clothing, the expression on her face, and her gestures all pointed to the fact that she didn't want to reenter the mainstream of life yet. She was obviously very sad and didn't attempt to hide it.

Seeing her shocked me, but I didn't let it show. I was suffering from the same grief because my husband had died not too long before. I understood her desire to creep away and quietly sit in a corner, shutting the world out. I knew that temptation.

I, too, would have just sat there, if God had not shown me I was taking the wrong way out. My life would have come to a dead end, with no future.

My attempt to escape from the world ended one day when I was very hungry for contact with my husband. Something drove me to his writing desk just to be where he had spent much time. As I rummaged through his papers, I found his diary, in which no date would ever be entered again. It fell open of its own accord. Aart, my husband, had flattened the pages to make it easier to write something.

It was a Bible verse! Had he read it one morning and wanted to remember it? I shall never know. I did know, however, that it was a special message for me. Beyond the concentration camp and death, my husband spoke to me for the last time. As I read, I realized that God was speaking to me. They were the words Jesus spoke to a man who had once struggled with the same problem I now had—longing for a beloved one who had died: "No one who puts his hand to the plow and looks back is fit for service in the kingdom of God" (Luke 9:62).

My thoughts flew back to when I said yes to Jesus Christ as a twelve-year-old. I saw myself again on that late summer evening years before. A small, insignificant human being had made an alliance with the everlasting God. And yet that was not presumptuous. I was answering his invitation: "Here I am! I stand at the door and knock. If anyone hears my voice and opens the door, I will go in and eat with him, and he with me" (Revelation 3:20). In answer to that knocking, I had opened the door of my heart in a childlike but very definite way.

I heard no sound of trumpets and saw no stars tumble from heaven. But the angels rejoiced at a sinner who had turned to God by accepting Jesus Christ. My heart had come to rest in a peace and security I had never known before. In the years since that day, all has not gone smoothly, but the conviction remains that I am a child of God!

That first yes to God was repeated at various stages in my life; for example, at our marriage. "In the future we want to serve you together, Lord. With our life. With our house. With everything you give us," we had said. Had I put my hand to the plough? Yes, beyond any doubt. The question that the Lord asked me now through this word of Scripture in Aart's diary was if I were still willing to continue along the road I had chosen to travel for him.

Did I dare do that—alone?

Going on meant having courage and believing that God had a future for me. I knew it was wrong to feel, at age twenty-five, that my life was over. But it was a difficult decision to be willing to be part of life again. Giving way to sorrow would be much easier. Living on memories was very attractive. But the price tag attached to that way of living was extremely expensive. For according to the verse in Aart's diary, it would mean being rejected for the Kingdom of God. The thought that I would be of no value for the one who had died for me was unbearable. My future would be doomed to senselessness. I thought of 2 Corinthians 5:15, which said that redeemed people should no longer live for themselves, but for him who died for them and was raised again.

So I chose him. I chose to look ahead to new possibilities—and the inevitable struggle. On that day I again said yes to God, to life, to myself. Looking back, I can say now that it was certainly the right choice. With him life became fascinating again!

Nini Boesman, Balloonist

"However hard life can be at times, there is always a future," said Mrs. Nini Boesman, the

Netherlands' most famous balloonist. Over a period of forty years she ascended in a balloon with her husband over five hundred times. When he died suddenly, she lost the courage to go up again. She decided to stop ballooning altogether.

Two years after his death, she took up her old sport again. "Young people are interested in balloon riding these days. It is necessary that older people share their knowledge," she said.

After the death of her husband, spiritual matters received more and more of her attention. Cooperating with a minister, she began to work on evangelical radio broadcasts. "I have finally come to realize, even though I still find it difficult at times, that my husband's death had a special purpose for me." The many reactions to the broadcasts are a stimulus for her to go on. "I realize now how much misery and distress there is in life. I hope to be able to help people a little by telling them of my experiences."

In her tastefully furnished home in The Hague we discussed the subject of widowhood. I asked her what gave her the courage to look forward again. The answer was a meeting with the Lord through his word. "It was just as if the Lord were saying to me, 'Do not think I have left you.' Indeed, he hadn't. In Hebrews 13:5 he says, 'Never will I leave you; never will I forsake you.'"

Thus Nini Boesman gained new courage and a desire to learn more about God so she could help others. God says in Jeremiah 49:11, "Your widows too can trust in me." Speaking about widows in Exodus 22:23 he said, "If . . . they cry out to me, I will certainly hear their cry."

Coping with Widowhood

Elisabeth Elliot's husband, Jim, was killed along with four other missionaries by the Auca Indians in Ecuador. After Jim died, Elisabeth startled the world by returning, with her little daughter, to live with the tribe that had killed her husband. She decided to live with her husband's murderers in order to continue the task that he and his colleagues had begun—reaching them for Christ.

Today there are Auca Indians who are evangelizing the surrounding tribes because of her work among them. The seed of God's word found fertile soil. It sprang forth with fruit. Why? Because a young widow had not let herself become paralyzed by the past. She kept her hand to the plow!

After Jim's death, she married again and became a widow a second time. In a magazine article entitled "The Ones Who Are Left"[1] she tells of six things that helped her cope with life as a single woman.

Be Still and Know that He Is God
This advice comes from Psalm 46, which begins by describing the sort of trouble from which God is our refuge: "Though the earth give way and the mountains fall into the heart of the sea,

though its waters roar and foam and the mountains quake with their surging." A widowed
woman experiences a similar overthrow of all
the security of her former life with her loved one.
Her whole world changes.

In this new, turbulent, uncertain situation,
God says, "I am your refuge, your strength, your
help. Whatever your loss, I am with you." Elisabeth notes, "We feel that we are alone, yet we
are not alone. . . . In the midst of all this hulla-
baloo we are commanded, 'Be still.' Be still and
know."

Being still means listening to Christ. Those
who do so will get their bearings and will not
suffocate in sorrow. Elisabeth writes,

> There are several ways of looking and listening
> . . . Bible reading and prayer are the obvious
> ones. Taking yourself by the scruff of the neck and
> setting aside a definite time in a definite place
> for deliberately looking at what God has said and
> listening to what he may have to say to you today
> is a good exercise. And if such exercises are
> seen as an obligation, they have the same power
> other obligations—cooking a meal, cleaning
> a bathroom, vacuuming a rug—have to save us
> from ourselves.

Give Thanks

Elisabeth thanked God, not for the fact that her
first husband was horribly murdered, nor that her
second husband was literally consumed by a
dreadful disease, but for his being there. In spite

of the storm he keeps the wheel of your ship of life firmly in his hands. The call in 1 Thessalonians 5:18 to give thanks in all circumstances doesn't mean thanking him for terrible things like war, famine, sickness, or death. *It does mean thanking him for the promise that God is with us in the midst of any of those calamities.* He will carry us through. It means trusting Jesus' words, "And surely I will be with you always, to the very end of the age" (Matthew 28:20).

Refuse to Give in to Self-pity
"I know of nothing more paralyzing, more deadly, than self-pity," Elisabeth writes. "It is a death that has no resurrection, a sinkhole from which no rescuing hand can drag you, because you have chosen to sink. But it must be refused."

She defines self-pity as being occupied all the time with the suffered loss. It is like putting the loss under a magnifying glass and blowing it up out of proportion. It is looking with envy on people who are better off and asking yourself, "Why should this happen to me?"

This doesn't mean we need to deny our loss. We can admit that we are suffering. But we mustn't consider our grief as unusual or as undeserved. Christ knows the weight and extent of our suffering because he has carried our sorrows (Isaiah 53:4). Therefore, we must nail our self-pity to the cross.

Accept Your Loneliness
Elisabeth continues, "When God takes a loved person from my life, it is in order to call me, in

a new way, to himself. It is therefore a vocation. It is in this sphere, for now anyway, that I am to learn of him ... to be brought to him. Loneliness is a stage (and, thank God, only a stage), when we are terribly aware of our own helplessness."

Accepting our loneliness clears the way for God to come to our aid.

Offer Your Loneliness to God

Something mysterious and miraculous transpires as soon as something is held up in our hands as a gift. He takes it from us, as Jesus took the little lunch when five thousand people were hungry (Matthew 14:14–21). He gives thanks for it and then, breaking it, transforms it for the good of others. Loneliness looks pretty paltry as a gift to offer to God—but then when you come to think of it, so does anything else we might offer. It needs transforming. Others looking at it would say exactly what the disciples said, "What's the good of that with such a crowd?" But it was none of their business what use the Son of God would make of it. And it is none of ours. It is ours only to give it.

Do Something for Someone Else

Elisabeth believes "there is nothing like definite, overt action to overcome the inertia of grief." The people around Jesus' death and burial exemplified this. Joseph of Arimathea, Nicodemus, and the women who knew the Lord intimately seized this opportunity to *do* something. The activities around his burial (Luke 23:50–56 and John 19:38–42) helped them lift themselves out of their deep sorrow.

The Bible gives other examples of widows who, in spite of their own sorrow, gave themselves to others. To their surprise, they experienced their own healing as a result of helping others. Think of Naomi's care for her widowed daughters-in-law, and what she received in return through one of these women, Ruth. Then Ruth found new happiness in life when she took care of her mother-in-law (Ruth 1–4). The widow from the small city of Zarephath owed her life (and her son's life) to the fact that she was prepared to share her last crumb of bread with someone else (1 Kings 17).

Mourning over a deceased loved one is natural. Jesus wept at the grave of his friend Lazarus (John 11:35–36). However, new insight and perspective are gained if we look at more than just the sad side of death. In 2 Corinthians 1:3–4 we read, "Praise be to the God and Father of our Lord Jesus Christ, the Father of compassion and the God of all comfort, who comforts us in all our troubles, so that we can comfort those in any trouble with the comfort we ourselves have received from God."

Comforters and encouragers are needed, because difficulties and uncertainties are abundant in human living. The best comforter is a person who knows what sorrow is like, but who also knows that God wants to help a person through the sorrow to a richer existence. Widows can fulfill a unique service in the kingdom of God.

After lifelong service in the temple, the widow Anna was privileged to tell the people in Jerusalem, who were expecting the Messiah, that he had been born (Luke 2:36–38). Mary of Jerusalem, generally considered to be a widow, held a prayer meeting in her home. The result was the release of Peter from prison.

Shortly after World War II, the director of a missionary organization visited many countries of the world hoping to inspire young people with his vision for missions and world evangelization. In one country he found only one person—a woman—willing to represent his organization. The responsibility was not a small one and the director did not hide the fact that he would rather appoint a man. Yet he gave her the assignment. "It is good this way" he said. "I suddenly realized that she is a widow."

NOTES
1. Elisabeth Elliot, "The Ones Who Are Left," *Christianity Today*, February 27, 1976, pages 7–8.

QUESTIONS FOR STUDY AND APPLICATION

1. Read Luke 9:57–62.
   a. In what context does Jesus speak about putting the hand to the plow?
   b. What are the consequences if a person looks back? Also consider Genesis 19:26 for your answer.

2. Read Job 1 and 2.
   a. Describe Job's reaction when death destroyed his family. What was his wife's reaction?
   b. What was the cause of the disasters in his life?
   c. According to Job 42:5–10, what was the final effect of all of this on Job's life?
   d. How can Job's experience be helpful to a widow?

3. The Psalms are excellent to read in times of sorrow. Psalm 40 portrays the great distress of David. What can you learn from it and apply?

4. Read the story of Joseph in Genesis 37, 39, and 41. In the light of Genesis 50:20 and Romans 8:28, what do you conclude?

5. Is there a situation in your life in which you need to consider Luke 9:62 again? What is the situation, and how can you apply the verse to it?

Extra study: Think about the six points mentioned by Elisabeth Elliot. How can they help you in a difficult situation you are facing (not necessarily widowhood)? Find cross-references for these points.

17

THERE IS HOPE FOR THE FUTURE

"You're nobody till somebody loves you," a deep male voice croons over the radio. "You're nobody till somebody cares."

These words poignantly speak to the woman who has just become a widow, for that is how she feels—worthless and not needed. This comes not only from losing her husband, but also from losing her status in society. Her personal identity suffers because her life had been so closely bound up with her husband's.

"A husband's position may also provide psychological support," writes Jane Gunther, widow of the well-known diplomat and author,

John Gunther. "Reflected glory may not seem attractive to women's libbers," she continues, "but it is true that a woman basks in her husband's success, is a part of it in the eyes of the world, and indeed, has often helped to create it."[1]

A widow asks herself, "Who am I, really? Do I have a personality of my own? What value am I anymore? Who am I, not as a wife or widow, but as a human being?"

The uncertainty of who she is affects not only the major areas of life, but the minor ones as well. Every widow knows how much courage it took to go to a meeting for the first time by herself. And the fact that society seems to cater to couples rather than to individuals makes it even more unbearable.

God Has a Plan for Each Widow

The answers to the widow's questions are found in God, the Creator of her plan of life. That is the first certainty she may discover: *there is a plan*!

Though her husband's death has changed her life drastically, it hasn't changed the fact that God has a plan for her life. Even the tragedy of the death fits into that plan. These sad days, too, were written in God's book "before one of them came to be" (Psalm 139:16).

It can't be expected that she will understand this immediately, but it can slowly become real to her wounded heart. The magnificent words of God to Jeremiah apply to the widow: " 'For I know the plans I have for you,' declares the Lord, 'plans to prosper you and not to harm you, plans to give you hope and a future' " (Jeremiah 29:11). With God there is always hope, always a future.

But, as with most of his promises, there is a condition: "You will seek me and find me when you seek me with all your heart" (Jeremiah 29:13).

The word *widow* and its derivations occur some eighty times in the Bible. God is deeply and genuinely concerned about the needs of widows. In fact, he is so deeply concerned that he measures our faith according to our attitude toward widows and orphans. James 1:27 says, "Religion that God our Father accepts as pure and faultless is this: to look after orphans and widows in their distress."

Tamar, the widow in Genesis 38, experienced God's help. Her widowhood meant returning to her parental home, a custom in the East. It would also mean a secluded existence, but Tamar refused to be sentenced to an idle life with no responsibilities. She took initiatives, which may seem strange to a Westerner and something which a Christian may not approve of, but God did not condemn her for doing it. With her unusual action, she claimed a justice that was being withheld from her by her society.

God notices any injustices done to widows. "He keeps the widow's boundaries intact," says Solomon in Proverbs 15:25. It is dangerous to take advantage of a widow, for you will have to give account of it to God. He has appointed himself to be "defender of widows" (Psalm 68:5). What an ineffable comfort!

Importance of Personal Decision-making

The Bible places the married woman under the responsibility of her husband. However, there is a separate law for the widow; she is accountable directly to God (Numbers 30:9). This means she is responsible for her own decisions.

How she uses her decision-making powers is very important. If she is wise, she will make as few decisions as possible immediately after her husband's death. The emotional shock may, for the time being, render her incapable of making sound decisions. Some widows, for example, move from their homes immediately, because they can't bear remaining there with many memories. Or they simply may wish to move closer to children or other relatives. Some immediately give away all their husband's clothes and personal possessions. Others find comfort in keeping them. Some of these decisions may be rash when viewed later from a less emotional stance. Widows should be careful in the early days.

It is often best not to take *all* the well-meaning advice from friends and relatives, at least for the present. This is not to say one shouldn't seek counsel, for the Bible strongly advocates this: "Listen to advice . . . and in the end you will be wise" (Proverbs 19:20). Especially make an effort to get advice from other widows.

In this new station in life, the widow has the unique opportunity to grow as a woman in spiritual capacity and in decision-making powers. If her husband helped her along these lines before his death, he left her something far more valuable than an insurance policy. For though financial security is of great value, a woman who does not know how to use it wisely, even though she has plenty of it, would be better off without it.

Two authors mentioned earlier, Katie Wiebe and Catherine Marshall, reveal how the necessity of making important decisions actually helped them grow as individuals. They discovered gifts within themselves that developed under pressure.

Catherine Marshall explained how a whole new world opened up to her when she edited a book of sermons her husband had written. She was introduced not only to the world of writing, but also to that of publishing. By having conversations with experts in these fields, she began developing more of her whole being.

She writes, "It made me experience something of the deep fulfillment and inner satisfaction that come to people who have found their vocation in life. But it was not as if I had completely adjusted myself to the loss. The great void was still there. I was still missing half of myself; but, nevertheless, it was as if I had found my own element."[2]

God Will Help

No task is too large to be tackled with God's help. And, conversely, nothing is too small to be used by him. "What is that in your hand?" the Lord asked Moses (Exodus 4:2). It was a simple shepherd's staff for prodding sheep, yet it became an instrument used to lead a whole nation out of a hostile country.

A widow in Elisha's time fell into enormous debt when her husband died. Because she couldn't pay, the creditor asked that her two sons become his slaves. The widow went to Elisha for help. As with Moses and the shepherd's staff, God again used a seemingly insignificant item for great purposes.

Elisha told her to get as many empty jars as possible from her neighbors. She did, and from the tiny portion of precious oil she had, jar after jar was filled to the brim. It didn't stop until she ran out of empty jars. All this oil provided far more money than needed to pay off the debt. She and her sons were able to live comfortably with the remainder. This is how God takes care of the widow who has faith.

Her faith was put into action when she was willing to indicate her need to others. If she had thought that her problems were so big that no

one, including God, could help her, then she
wouldn't have gotten the empty jars. But because she asked, not only a prophet, but also all
her friends came to her assistance.

"The Lord . . . sustains the fatherless and the
widow" (Psalm 146:9). Indeed! But he often does
it through people. It takes wise insight to know
the difference between right and wrong depen-
dency; between sharing your needs with others
and needlessly bothering them; between relying on people or relying on God.

Proper balance needs to be learned. It isn't
achieved at once, but gradually. It is learned by
testing our experiences with God's word and allowing his word to be the norm for our lives. If
a woman excludes the possibilities of the utili-
zation of small things and the help of others, she
builds on a very narrow foundation.

The Widows in Jesus' Life

Widows played a large part in Jesus' life on earth.
One of the two people who saw him when he
was presented to God in the temple was Anna,
a widow. She became the herald of the Messiah
(Luke 2:21–33).

Years later, Jesus saw a widow burying her
only son. It moved him extraordinarily. "Don't
cry," he said, then raised the boy from the grave
(Luke 7:11–17). He didn't want this woman to
have sorrow upon sorrow.

As there was a widow at the beginning of

his earthly life, so was there one at the end. His last deed on the cross was to take care of a widow. He didn't say, "It is finished," until he had taken care of his own mother, Mary. In the presence of everyone there, he asked the disciple whom he loved the most to take care of his mother. "From that time on, this disciple took her into his home" (John 19:25–27). A very simple but touching statement! God finished his task on earth by taking care of a widow.

Later, in Acts 1:14, Mary is listed among the disciples. She has a new purpose in life—that of devoting herself to the service of God.

Many widows have found this type of service to be their deepest joy. Some live out their lives accomplishing a more common task. Others remarry. But whatever the task, it is secondary; the important matter is accomplishing God's plan for her life. And if she is moving forward with him, step by step, she can rest assured she will arrive at the proper destination. God will lead her not only to a future in which she will discover her own identity, but to one in which she is secure.

It is a future with hope!

NOTES

1. Jane Gunther, *Reader's Digest*, September 1975, page 106.
2. Catherine Marshall, *This Is My Life* (*Dit Is Mijn Leven*), (Baarn, The Netherlands: Bosch & Keuning N.V.), page 48.

QUESTIONS FOR STUDY AND APPLICATION

1. The book of Ruth tells about three widows. Read this book in conjunction with 1 Timothy 5:3–16.
   a. Who do you feel was the most unhappy of the three widows? Why?
   b. What did Naomi do to find new meaning for life?
   c. What lessons can you learn from Ruth about others, about a second marriage, and about God?

2. How does the story of the widow in 2 Kings 4 prove that widows can rightly trust in God? What can every widow learn from this chapter?

3. How would you describe the faith and courage of the widow of Zarephath, as revealed in 1 Kings 17?

4. Read Acts 8:1 and 12:1–19. What was the spiritual atmosphere at the time Mary of Jerusalem placed her home at the disposal of God? What were the results of her act?

5. What do the following verses say about God's attitude and thoughts regarding widows? Exodus 22:22–24; Deuteronomy 10:18, 26:12, 27:19; Jeremiah 7:5–7; James 1:27

Extra study: List all the widows from the Bible

who are discussed in the chapters on widow-hood. What do you find remarkable in each life? What does this say to you about God and Jesus? Perhaps you know some widows with whom you could share the results of this study.

18

THE BEST IS YET TO COME

Recently I sat captivated in front of my television set watching a documentary about the endless versatility of the human brain. Scientists say we have far more possibilities at our disposal than we presently realize. The problem is to find how we can sufficiently make use of them.

One of the scientists on the program said that the largest computer is nothing more than a "quick idiot" compared with the human intellect. In comparison with our brain cell information exchange system, a telephone exchange is a "stupid thing." One neuron cell can accomplish more connections a day than all the telephone exchanges in the world put together. A person's brain contains many million neuron cells, and all have connections with each other. Such a capacity results in trillions and trillions of possibilities!

It is a humiliating thought that we have hardly begun utilizing our potential. A newborn child is the nearest to perfection, yet our brain can grow and develop even into old age.

After I turned off the television, I prayed that I would make better use of what I have already learned. But in light of the documentary, I could expect that *the best is yet to come*.

The Sadness of Physical Immaturity

The Bible teaches that the most fascinating aspect of creation is growth. God gave all living creatures the capacity to grow and change. He provided innumerable possibilities to allow us to develop and to bear fruit.

In the provincial Dutch town where I grew up, there was a boy, Peter, whom I will never forget. It is not because of anything special he did, or because he was handsome or strong or talented. Unfortunately, Peter attracted attention because he was a dwarf.

I met this boy with the short legs and large head each morning on my way to school. Why do I still think of him? Because he became a symbol of the sadness of immaturity.

I wonder how many tears this boy must have shed because he was different than other people. I think of his parents and how shocked they must have been when the doctors told them their beloved son would never mature physically.

Perhaps as the years passed, that sadness grew into bitterness, because Peter's deficient body could not be hidden from people.

The Sadness of Spiritual Immaturity

The thought of the tears of Peter and his parents makes me think of the tears of God. However startling a physical deformity may be, there is something far worse—spiritual immaturity. To see a person remain spiritually immature must pain God so very much because of his love for us. And there are many who do not grow: "There has been enough time for you to be teachers— yet you still need someone to teach you the first lessons of God's message. Instead of eating solid food, you still have to drink milk. Anyone who has to drink milk is still a child without any experience in the matter of right and wrong" (Hebrews 5:12–13, *Good News for Modern Man*).

How many Christians are spiritual dwarfs? That is precisely what we are if we don't keep growing mentally and spiritually, if we don't tap the inexhaustible resources at our disposal. Then we are the cause of God's tears.

Biblical Examples of Growth

Jesus was a splendid example of proper growth: "And Jesus increased in wisdom (in broad and full understanding), and in stature and years, and in favor with God and man" (Luke 2:52, AMP). This shows us the development of the whole person, as desired by God—intellectual, physical, spiritual, and social. It encompasses growth in regard to yourself, your fellowman, and God.

Samuel, Joseph, and John became great men in the history of the kingdom of God. "And the boy Samuel continued to grow in stature and in favor with the Lord and with men" (1 Samuel 2:26). Joseph's intellectual growth was coupled with his physical, social, and spiritual growth. John the Baptist "grew and became strong in spirit" (Luke 1:80).

Potential of Spiritual Growth

In the field of our intellectual capacities, there are unimaginable heights that we haven't yet reached. Spiritually, this is even more true. Jesus says no less than "Be perfect, therefore, as your heavenly Father is perfect" (Matthew 5:48). The word *perfect* here means full grown, mature in godly understanding and character.

Paul talks about us growing "until we all reach unity in the faith and in the knowledge of the Son of God and become mature, attaining to the whole measure of the fullness of Christ" (Ephesians 4:13).

We do not attain spiritual maturity all at once, however. That would be unnatural. "I would feel cheated," a father said to me, "if my young son, by some miracle, became an adult instantly. I want to enjoy every phase of his development. I want to help him with it."

This is also true in our spiritual development; our heavenly Father wants to help us with it. He doesn't expect any more of us than can take place *step by step*!

The Necessity of Growth

Jesus' example proves that growth is necessary. He also shows us that spiritual growth takes place best in a close relationship with God. As a twelve-year-old boy he amazed his parents and the religious teachers because of his hunger for the things of God. He was so desirous to learn that he asked intelligent questions of learned theologians (Luke 2:41–50). These things were his food (John 4:34). Jesus grew into a man who included God in the daily reality of living. In order to pray uninterrupted, he met with God in the quietness of dawn. When important decisions had to be made, such as choosing the disciples, he made them after prolonged prayer (Luke 6:12–13).

How to Grow Spiritually

Our growth depends upon our desire for the spiritual milk of the word (1 Peter 2:2). Enfolded in his love, we should grow up in every way and in all things toward Christ (Ephesians 4:15).

The food and cosmetic industries spend prodigious amounts of money on advertising to convince us that what we eat and the way we take care of ourselves determine who we are. In our mental and spiritual life, this is even more significant. With what do we feed ourselves? (What do we read? What occupies our thoughts and conversations? How do we spend our spare time?) Retaining a spiritual posture in a world that is getting increasingly more materialistic, egoistic, and perverse is difficult, indeed.

But we have help—God's word and his Holy Spirit. They will help determine our daily life's pattern. They will inform and guide us. They will correct us as well and enable us to grow into better balanced Christians. We shall be prepared for our task and equipped for every good work (2 Timothy 3:16–17). We shall bring honor to the name of God and with that fulfill the purpose of our lives.

The Bible compares a Christian to a fruit tree. The tree's purpose is ultimately to bear fruit. It is important that its roots are fed with water and that its leaves breathe pure air, but its fruitfulness is greatly dependent upon how well it reacts to resistance and adversity. How does it react to heat, freezing temperatures, and storms? Is its inner strength such that it doesn't succumb under difficulties? If so, fruit is ensured.

Jesus learned from suffering (Hebrews 5:8). He endured the cross and shame because he kept looking at the joy that lay ahead for him. He lived with the thought that *the best is yet to come.*

God allows suffering in humanity in order that we grow in character. He has also promised that the difficulties will not be beyond our capacity to handle, and neither will they last indefinitely (1 Corinthians 10:13). If we follow Jesus' example in times of trouble, we need not grow weary or fainthearted (Hebrews 12:2–3).

Choosing growth and maturity is choosing adventure. Living with God is truly an adventure. "Maturity is often mistaken for dullness. That's why you often see such an immature style of life," says a female psychologist who works with young women.

People who have tasted what growth means and what it can lead to think differently. They want to move ahead and continue developing. Because they choose to grow, they choose to follow God.

Live by Priorities

The way to start developing in the right direction is to start living with priorities. Give priority to the things that need your attention first. This will help you make better use of your time. Matters of minor importance should get the attention they deserve—minor. It is good to set attainable goals and check them from time to time to see if you are achieving them.

The president of a large company once said

to an efficiency expert, "I don't function as well as I know I could. I do not need to know more, but I must learn how to do more. If you can give me something that stimulates me to do the things I already know to do, I will reward you for your advice."

The expert handed him a sheet of paper and said, "Write down the six most important tasks you have to do tomorrow. Number them in order of importance. The first thing in the morning begin working on number one. Work on it until you complete it. Then do point two, and so forth. Do this until closing time. If you don't complete all six points in this way, then you wouldn't have completed them in any other way either. But this way you will have not only done a full day's work, but you will have done the most important things. Work every day in this manner. Try it for as long as you like and send me a check for the amount you feel this advice was worth."

A few weeks later the expert received a check for an enormous amount of money, plus a letter in which the businessman said that this was the greatest lesson he had ever learned.[1]

Living with priorities is necessary not only for businessmen; a woman who chooses to mature spiritually will also have to organize her life by planning her priorities. You can ask yourself what are the most important things you want to accomplish in the next three to six months. The purpose is to get insight on the reality of your life. What is necessary in your relationship with

God? What needs are there in your family, job, or education? Should you plan more time for relaxation and exercise?

What strong character qualities could you make better use of? What weak ones need development? Do you want to read some books or take a class?

With this book you have a perfect opportunity for growth by answering the questions at the end of each chapter. A few weeks from now, see what has resulted from your personal application of your answers.

Words like *priorities* and *setting goals* have to do with planning and organization. Perhaps you think they sound chilly and businesslike and belong in a man's world. But why shouldn't things that serve a man in life also serve a woman?

We do need to reexamine our lives now and then and perhaps readjust our goals. Each phase of life offers a specific challenge to grow in the deepest purpose of our life—to glorify God.

Yes, the best is yet to come, when we shall experience what is written in 1 Corinthians 2:9–

> No eye has seen, no ear has heard, no mind has conceived, what God has prepared for those who love him.

NOTES
1. R. Alec Mackenzie, *The Time Trap* (Amacom, 1972), pages 38–39.

QUESTIONS FOR STUDY AND APPLICATION

1. Write down everything you discover about growth in the following verses: Luke 8:15, Colossians 1:9–11, 1 Peter 2:2, 2 Peter 3:18.

2. Which fruit are identified in Galatians 5:22 and Philippians 1:9–11?

3. Read John 15:5. Who is responsible if we bear fruit, and why?

4. What do Hebrews 5:8 and James 1:2–4 teach in connection with bearing spiritual fruit?

5. Read Ephesians 4:13–15 and Hebrews 5:12–14 in as many translations as you can. Write down what you learned about spiritual growth.

6. How should this study influence your growth? Be personal and practical.

Extra study: Examine once more all of the applications you made in connection with each chapter of this book. Perhaps you want to make a list of those things you intended to do but haven't done yet. Put in order of their priority all of the things you want to put into practice. Then begin doing them, one by one.

APPENDIX A
HOW TO HAVE A QUIET TIME

It is a miracle in itself that God allows an individual to fellowship with him in person. To know that he desires this and that it brings joy to his heart cannot help but lead us to deep reflection—and *action*.

If chapter three ("Finding God's Will") stirred your desire to spend daily time with God, here are some suggestions to help you develop this habit.

For most people, the best time to meet with God is at the beginning of the day. Their minds are fresh, and the day lies unspoiled before them. If, however, for practical reasons you must choose another time, it is still wise to do it as early in the day as possible. Be sure to select a time when you can spend unhurried and uninterrupted moments in God's presence.

Plan for your quiet time the night before. Don't go to bed so late that you will not be fresh for your meeting with God. Set your clock earlier than you normally get up.

Find a place where you can go regularly. Make sure you are alone.

The length of your quiet time is not as important as being consistent in having it. I suggest beginning with from seven to ten minutes each day.

Remember that you are in God's presence. Concentrate your first thoughts on him. Thank him for a good night of rest. Pray that your heart will be open to his truth and that your mind will be fresh and alert to his voice, as expressed in Psalm 119:18—"Open my eyes that I may see wonderful things in your law."

After this, read from your Bible for a few minutes, being confident that God will speak to you through his word. Read a brief portion— perhaps a chapter, or only a few verses.

Mark's Gospel is good to begin with. You could read John's Gospel next, then the rest of the New Testament and the Psalms. Read carefully, word for word, chapter after chapter, as the days and weeks go by. If your thoughts wander, remember that you are meeting with the one who loves you unreservedly.

Try to discover the main thought in what you read. Keep it in your mind throughout the day so you can concentrate on it and review it. Ask yourself, *How can this one thought influence my life today?* This is the purpose of God's word— *to change our lives*.

Questions such as the following will help you apply the word to your life as you read.

Is there an example I can follow?

Is there a command I should obey?

Is there a mistake to avoid?

Is there a sin I should abstain from?

Is there a promise I can claim?

Those who want a more simple approach are offered a good alternative by Paul's words in Acts 9:5–6 (AMP)—"Who are you, Lord? . . . What do you desire me to do?"

After God has spoken to you through the Scriptures, you should talk to him in prayer.

These five suggestions for prayer may be helpful.

Begin your prayer time with *adoration*. Fix your thoughts on God, not yourself. You can adore and worship him because of his love, his holiness, his power, his faithfulness, and many other aspects of his character.

Confession comes next. David wrote that God will hear us after we have confessed our sins (Psalm 32:5). Confession of sin is required if we expect to receive answers to prayer. Is there anything you must confess so your contact with him will not be blocked?

Thanksgiving is the next component of prayer. Thank God for all the good things he has given you—your salvation, his word, the opportunity to speak to him in prayer, his blessing on your work, your family, your friends, and many other gifts.

Intercession is praying for others—family and friends, pastors and missionaries, government leaders, and individuals who have not come to faith in Christ.

A good way to conclude is *prayer for yourself*. Freely tell God what is on your heart. Share your deepest thoughts with him. He wants to be involved in every aspect of your life. No petition is too great or too small for him to answer, so pray specifically. Present your clearly defined requests to him and don't forget to thank him for his answers.

As you follow these suggestions day by day, ten minutes may not be enough time. You may want to lengthen the amount of time you spend with God as your fellowship with him deepens.

APPENDIX B
SUGGESTIONS FOR DISCUSSION GROUPS

I feel, as many do, that fruitful discussion results when small groups of people share what they have discovered in their personal Bible study. The following suggestions will be helpful for those interested in leading a Bible study group.

1. *Preparation for a discussion group*
   a. Invite people of about the same age and interests. In this way you achieve clear communication and understanding.
   b. A small group of about six people is ideal. If there are more than ten who wish to participate, form a second group. In this way, the number is large enough for a profitable discussion, but small enough for everyone to join in.
   c. Discuss beforehand how often you wish to meet. Start, for instance, with four to six times. Since each chapter of this book forms a complete study within itself, you can choose chapters that are of the most interest to you. After meeting a few times, you can decide if you desire to continue, and for how long.
   d. Ask each participant to purchase a copy of the book, to study the chapter to be discussed and answer the questions at home beforehand. This will assure that the discussion is the result of personal study. You will also have less trouble sticking to the subject.

e. Encourage each group member to do her utmost to attend each meeting.

f. Meet in a pleasant atmosphere. Be sure the room is well ventilated and the temperature is comfortable. If too warm or too cool, people will not be at ease. Also be sure that no one has to look into a bright light. The success of your discussion often depends on matters like these.

g. Plan the seating arrangement ahead of time. It might be best to sit in a circle. Plan any other details carefully so you can begin and end on time.

2. *Personal preparation for the leader*

a. Pray for yourself and for each member of the group. Pray that Christ will speak through his word to every person present. Ask the Holy Spirit to make you sensitive to the needs of the people in your group.

b. Consider yourself a regular member of the group, but one whose task it is to see that all points of the study are discussed and that the discussion proceeds pleasantly.

c. Be sure you spend sufficient time doing the study yourself. Since questions are already given at the end of the chapters, it should not be too difficult to lead a discussion.

d. As you prepare, consider which points you wish to emphasize. Put those points before the group in the form of questions that stimulate thinking, that can be answered from the Scriptures, and that apply to practical daily living. Avoid questions that can be answered with a simple yes or no. Begin questions by asking who, what, where, why, and how.

e. Summarize each point that is discussed, or have someone in the group do it before you go on to the next question.

f. Although group members can take turns leading, it is good for the same person to do it a number of times in order to get experience.

3. *During the discussion*

a. Maintain a relaxed, informal atmosphere which allows people to get to know one another.

b. Consider each question for its own value. Some will require only a short answer, while others will need to be enlarged upon.

c. Keep the questions general. If you do direct a specific question to an individual for a particular reason, be sure you have her permission to do so ahead of time.

d. Allow sufficient time for those in the group to answer. Do not be afraid of silences. If necessary, repeat the question in a natural and easy manner.

e. Help the shy ones participate. For instance, have them read the question or appropriate verse aloud. People who talk easily in a group sometimes have to be restrained or they will dominate the discussion.

f. Be convinced that each person can make a valid contribution. Show you appreciate each contribution, whether or not it is to the point. If the answer is wrong, ask what others think.

g. If a question is asked by someone in the group, let others attempt to answer it before you do. The leader of the group shouldn't dominate either! In an ideal discussion group, the members interact with each other as well as with the leader.

h. If desired, you can use part of the discussion time for praying together. However, this should be done with tact. If some would rather not, don't pray as a group until a later time when they do want to have group prayer.

i. Keep your objective of changed lives in view. Your goal is not just to increase in knowledge, but to apply the word and its principles to daily living.